Bob Marley
The Complete Annotated Bibliography

Copyright © 2009 by Joseph Jurgensen

All rights reserved. No part of this book may be reproduced in any form or by electronic or mechanical means, including information storage and retrieval systems, without permission in writing from the publisher, except by a reviewer who may quote brief passages in a review.

Published by *Haras Publishing*

Prospect, KY

www.jahcoustic.com

Front and back photographs by Adrian Judy

Printed and bound in the United States of America

ISBN-13: 978-0-578-03940-4

First Edition

Bob Marley

The Complete Annotated Bibliography

By Joe Jurgensen

Foreword by Roger Steffens

Haras Publishing

Contents

Acknowledgments v

Foreword vii

Introduction ix

1. English Biographies 1

2. Discographies and Song Guides 43

3. Photography 57

4. Illustration 69

5. Non-English Biographies 77

6. Songbooks 119

7. Books featuring Bob Marley on the cover 133

Index 153

Give Thanks

This book would not have been possible without the help of many friends from around the world. I give special thanks to everybody who helped me with book information, cover scans and helping me sort through the abundance of non English books. First and foremost Roger Steffens; Brother RoJAH, I can't thank you enough for everything you have done and helped me with over the years. You are a great friend and a kind soul and your generosity is second to NONE! Huge thanks to my mate Glen Lockley. Glen you are a true Marley Apostle and thoughtful friend, many thanks for all of your help with this book and everything else Wailers related. A special thanks to all of the following friends, for without their help this book would not be what it is: Stephen Davis, Mike Meyers, Kevin Mac Donnell, Bruno Blum, Marco Virgona, Mike van der Linde, Chris Charlesworth, Gael Doyen, Ivan Serra, CC Smith, Robert Roskind, Ellen Kohlings, +C Chris Wright, Raul Fabio Vega Perez, Christian Lacoste, Adrian Judy, Lowell Taubman MD, Horace Campbell, John Masouri, David Moskowitz, Fabio Braghieri, Klaus Boehmer, Nadia Montanari, Fred Perry, Jesse Watson, Greg MacAyeal from Northwestern University Music Library, Karl Pitterson, Mariah Fox, Joe Schenkman, Michael Tsiparis, Frank Derks, Nicole Bryan from the NLJ, Augustos Magege, Allen Mounsey, Carol Haile Selassie, Fikisha Cumbo, Vivien Goldman, Kim Gottlieb-Walker, Jeremy Collingwood and anybody else I forgot to add. If I missed you please forgive me and send an email telling me to wise up. I will be sure to include you in future editions. Thanks to all of the authors, photographers, illustrators and publishers who have devoted time, energy, money and love to help spread the message and story of Bob Marley. You have provided us fans with fascinating and informative reads.

Many blessings and much respect goes to Peter Tosh and the Peter Tosh Estate.

And last but not least Bob Marley for writing, singing and recording the greatest, most important songs our world has ever heard. Special thanks to all of The Wailers for providing the best music to those incredible songs: Peter, Bunny, Bob, Aston, Carly, Al, Junior, Seeco, Tyrone, Wya, Donald, Touter, Joe and the I-Threes: Judy, Marcia and Rita.

Much love to my family: my mom and editor Patty Jurgensen, my dad Jerry Jurgensen, my in-laws John and Cathy Vinson, my children and Marley lovers Tyler, Samuel and Savannah. BUT I give the most love and thanks to my wonderful and understanding wife Sarah. Thanks baby, I Love you!

ONE LOVE

Black and white Turkish promo post card for Before the Legend
Bilge Kultar Sanat 2006   3.75" x 5.75"

Foreword

Books are like lovers.

Like an intriguingly dressed woman, book covers are meant first and foremost, to attract attention. Once met, we look at the contents of books to see how many concurrences there are between our own interests and whatever tempting secrets the book promises to reveal to us.

The more time we spend with them, the more they become part of our lives. And in the case of a successful relationship, when we have devoured the contents of the book and found it acceptable, we want it to remain part of our lives, a friend between covers, placed on a shelf or beside a bed, to retain access whenever the need moves us. Sometimes the initially bright promise of a glossy package is diminished by an in-depth delving into its contents, in which case, it can be cast aside with regret, like a broken promise. But the most satisfying ones are those that you want to keep around you, for reference and refreshment, and the reminder of the good hours you spent together. We introduce books that we love to our friends in the hope that others will find our literary partners worthy too.

But in an era of overwhelming choices, we also look for guidance – in these days, perhaps from MatchFace or other websites linking people of similar tastes – or in the rapidly diminishing pages of a New York Times Book Review or magazine that caters to a reading public, helping us sort through the chaff for the few outstanding creations that merit our attention.

My friend Joe Jurgensen is one of those insatiable readers who overstands that not every voice is worth listening to, especially on a subject that has garnered such an unprecedented international audience as the life and works of the Caribbean singer-cum-prophet, Bob Marley. Through the continuous spread of his records, cds, film and videos, the three-decades-gone Marley has fulfilled his own prophecy about reggae music – it, and he, just keep getting bigger and bigger, as the value of his cries to conscience continues to reverberate around the globe. He has given voice to the voiceless, hope to the hopeless, identifying oppressors and the means to surmount their depredations. The fact that his moral wisdom touches all souls is manifestly evident in these pages on which my friend Joe outlines the hundreds of volumes that have been written about the Sage of Nine Mile, in many languages and published on every continent. How then, to wade through this tsunami of information? That was the task Joe set for himself over five years ago, resulting in the book you now hold. In it you will find descriptions of all the Marleyphile books his incredible research has uncovered, with his notes on their contents and relative worth, a task as remarkable for its weighty labor as it is for its illuminating result.

Herein are books for lovers and thinkers and collectors and casual fans as well. Some are Jack Webb-like just-the-facts-ma'am overviews such as 2009's Taschen Icon series release *Marley* and my own collaboration with Leroy Jodie Pierson that gives details of every song recorded by Bunny, Bob and Peter, the original trio – *Bob Marley and the Wailers: The Definitive Discography*. Others provide a dependably factual history of his life and times, such as Stephen Davis' groundbreaking early '80s biography, called simply *Bob Marley*, tapping recent memories of those closest to him; Chris Salewicz's eloquent *Songs of Freedom*, released in conjunction with the early '90s box set of the same name, and his recent *Bob Marley: The Untold Story*; and the monumental review of the recordings-in-progress, *Wailing Blues, The Story of Bob Marley's Wailers*, written by John Masouri over a nine year period with the Wailers' band leader, Aston "Family Man" Barrett.

For those who love all things Marley there are lavish art-rich tomes like Tony Medina and Jesse Joshua Watson's ostensible children's book, *I and I: Bob Marley*, with its lustrous paintings of key moments in Bob's life; and the massive leather bound collectors edition of Kate Simon's brilliant photographic/oral history *Rebel Music*, well worth its $400 price tag.

Books in Japanese, German, Spanish, Arabic and Korean feature in these pages as well. Although the Wailers were never honored in Jamaica until they had become stars overseas, it is clear now that they knew the accuracy of their own prophecy in 1970 when they sang, "the stone that the builder refuse shall be the head corner stone." Joe Jurgensen's livication to compiling the evidence of Marley's (and the Wailers') worldwide impact is a unique contribution to the ongoing documentation of the most important musical artist of the twentieth century. "I love books," Joe says, "the smell, the feel, the enjoyment they bring. They last forever. Some editions become incredible collectors' items. People cherish first editions, autographed volumes, and hard covers." The idea of curling up with a good computer is no substitute for a gorgeous book.

-Roger Steffens, Echo Park, CA, October, 24, 2009

Roger Steffens is known worldwide as one of the foremost authorities on Bob Marley and The Wailers and reggae music. He has authored several books, countless magazine articles, and dozens of album liner notes. He has produced several albums, including *The Complete Bob Marley & The Wailers* JAD set and a three disc *Peter Tosh live and acoustic set*. Steffens is a long time actor, radio broadcaster, photographer and lecturer. He regularly tours his *Life of Bob Marley* presentation, speaks frequently at the Rock and Roll Hall of Fame, and contributes to VH1 specials. He was the founding editor of *The Beat* reggae magazine and co-host of the Reggae Beat radio show on KCRW. Roger Steffens lives in Los Angeles where he maintains the world's largest archive of Bob Marley, Wailers and Reggae memorabilia.

Introduction

I've been collecting Bob Marley and reggae memorabilia for many years and books have always been an integral part of my collection. I own hundreds of books about Bob Marley and feel that a proper bibliography has never been published. This book is attempting to fill that void or at the very least lay a solid foundation that can be built on in the years to come. My objective of it is to serve not only as a resource guide for collectors but also act as nice visual treat for the casual Bob Marley or reggae fan. I have attempted to document each book and provide basic but vital information. You may notice that, contrary to its title, this book is far from complete. In fact any time you see a '?' that means I have not been able to verify or obtain a particular piece of information. I hope that this first Bob Marley bibliography will be used as a springboard to fill in those blanks and that the next edition will live up to its title. I also hope that the next edition will be in color because the many vivid covers and photos need to be seen in color to be truly appreciated.

I have divided the books into seven categories. The first and most abundant category is English Biographies, followed by Discographies and Song Guides, Photography, Illustration, Non-English Biographies, Songbooks and finally books that feature Marley on the cover but are not devoted to him. Foreign language books will be found in their respective category unless it is a biography or a lyric book. With a few exceptions, every volume included in this work contains an International Standard Book Number, or ISBN, a 10 or 13 digit number that uniquely identifies books and book like products published internationally. Starting in 2007 all newly issued ISBNs contained 13 digits. Publishers, though, often purchased ISBNs in bulk so you will see some books published after 2007 with 10 digits ISBNs. I chose to include some books that do not have an ISBN because it was obvious that they were published in the spirit of a book, as opposed to a magazine, fanzine or promotional booklet, and are therefore appropriate for inclusion. Many editions do not list an ISBN.

The book information is divided into nine parts: **1)** title; **2)** author/authors; **3)** publisher location; **4)** publisher; **5)** year published; **6)** 10 or 13 ISBN; **7)** number of pages; **8)** price, if printed on the book or stated by publisher; **9)** description of the book such as edition, binding, size, synopsis and any additional pertinent information.

It should be noted that I own a copy of almost, but not every book included. I have made every effort to get accurate and complete information about each book but I simply can't guarantee the information to be 100% error-free for the books I don't own. I would be grateful if you would submit to me any missing information or inaccuracies to me so I can make the corrections for future editions.

It should also be noted that the information presented is not formatted in the typical MLA bibliography style. For example, I cite countries and states as well as the city of publication. I organized the bibliography chronologically, similar to a typical descriptive collector's bibliography. Some common abbreviations used throughout this book are: PB= paperback, HC= hardcover, trans. = translation and ed. = edition. A book is considered a reprint if the publisher used the same plates and made no changes to the text. It is considered a new or revised edition if changes to the text have been made or updates have been added. Some of the book sizes have been rounded to the nearest quarter inch. The majority of the prices listed are prices that are printed on the book. The few exceptions are prices that the publishers provided.

Future editions of this bibliography will contain much more detail as it becomes available. Again, this book is intended to be just a basic starting point but one that needed to be published in order for future editions to be more accurate and complete. The title *The Complete Bibliography* is more of a goal than a statement of fact.

-Joe Jurgensen

Biographies

More biographies have been published about Bob Marley than books in any of the other sections. Since the first biography in 1976, we have seen at least one new one hit the market almost every year. Although not every book listed in this chapter may be considered a true biography, such as *In His Words,* its inclusion is more appropriate for this section than any other. While many of these biographies have only had one edition some, such as *Catch a Fire: The Life of Bob Marley* by Timothy White, and *Bob Marley* by Stephen Davis, have seen several editions. The list of biographies grows larger by the year and by the looks of things shows no sign of slowing down. It is rumored that there are still several yet to be published.

Black and white advert for Catch a Fire: The Life of Bob Marley, Corgi 1984
From a UK Trade Paper 5.25" x 7.25"

Title: *Bob Marley: Music Myth & The Rastas*
Author: Henderson Dalrymple
Place of Publication: Middlesex, UK
Publisher: Carib-Arawak Publishers Ltd.
Year: 1976: **ISBN-10:** None
Pages: 77: **Price:** .50 p UK
Description: Paperback with color pictorial wrappers, 8.25" x 5.75". Note: The first published biography about Bob Marley. It offers a look at Marley's life from an African point of view. Includes black and white photos, lyrics to songs and a lesson in Rastafari. This is a stapled book with a heavy cardstock cover.

Title: *Bob Marley: The Roots of Reggae*
Author(s): Cathy McKnight and John Tobler
Place of Publication: London, UK
Publisher: A Star Book Published by paperback division of W.H. Allen & Co.
Year: 1977: **ISBN-10:** 0352396229
Pages: 160: **Price:** .75 p UK; $2.75 Australia; $2.30 New Zealand; 80 c Malta
Description: Paperback with color pictorial wrappers, 4.25" x 7". Note: The first published English biography with an ISBN. It contains a brief biography and discography. Illustrated with black and white photos.

Title: *No Woman No Cry: The Life of Bob Marley*
Author: DR. Gabriel Kingsley Osei
Place of Publication: London, UK
Publisher: The African Publication Society
Year: 1981: **ISBN:** None
Pages: 39: **Price:** None Listed
Description: Paperback with color pictorial wrappers, 8.25" x 5.5". Note: A short biography about the life of Marley illustrated with black and white photos. This is a stapled book with a cardstock cover.

Title: *Bob Marley Lives: Rasta, Reggae And Resistance*
Author: Horace Campbell
Place of Publication: Dar es Salaam, Tanzania
Publisher: Tackey BCI
Year: 1982: **ISBN:** None
Pages: 21: **Price:** None Listed
Description: Paperback with pictorial wrappers, 6.75" x 9.25". Note: Transcriptions of song lyrics including Survival, Zimbabwe, War, Africa Unite and Redemption Song

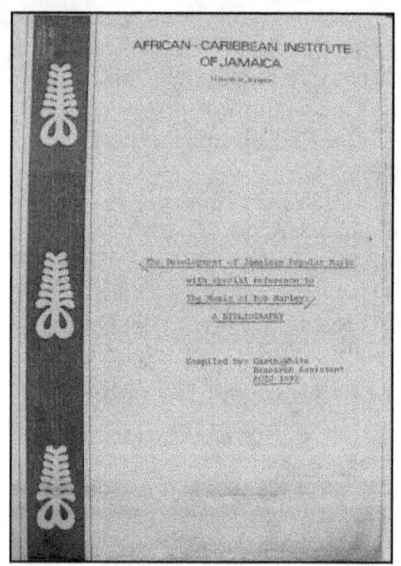

Title: *The Development of Jamaican Popular music with special reference to The Music of Bob Marley / A Bibliography*
Author: Garth White
Place of Publication: Kingston, Jamaica
Publisher: African-Caribbean Institute of Jamaica
Year: 1982: **ISBN:** None
Pages: 49: **Price:** None Listed
Description: Paperback with printed wrappers, 7.25" x 10.5". Note: A comprehensive list of material relevant to the study of Jamaican popular music with focus on the music of Bob Marley.

Title: *Bob Marley*
Author: Stephen Davis
Place of Publication: London, UK
Publisher: Arthur Baker Limited
Year: 1983: **ISBN-10:** 0213168553
Pages: 248: **Price:** [?]
Description: First UK edition, hardcover, full orange cloth, gilt, in color pictorial dust jacket, 6.25" x 9.25". Note: One of the first in depth biographies about Marley and is illustrated with several black and white photos. It still stands the test of time and has seen many new editions and printings throughout the world. Regarded by many as the best biography written about Bob Marley.

Title: *Bob Marley*
Author: Stephen Davis
Place of Publication: London, UK
Publisher: Arthur Baker Limited
Year: 1983: **ISBN-10:** 0213168596
Pages: 248: **Price:** £5.95 UK
Description: First UK edition, paperback with color pictorial wrappers, 6.25" x 9.25". Note: One of the first in depth biographies about Marley and is illustrated with several black and white photos. This book has 11 English printings. Regarded by many as the best biography written about Bob Marley.

Title: *Catch a Fire: The Life of Bob Marley*
Author: Timothy White
Place of Publication: London, UK
Publisher: Elm Tree Books
Year: 1983: **ISBN-10:** 0241109566
Pages: 380: **Price:** [?]
Description: First UK edition, hardcover, full black cloth, gilt, in color pictorial dust jacket, 6.25" x 9.25". Note: This comprehensive history of Bob Marley has seen more printings and revisions than any other biography. It has 16 English printings with five total editions. It covers his life along with some Caribbean history and offers the reader a detailed album list. Illustrated with several black and white photos.

Title: *Catch a Fire: The Life of Bob Marley*
Author: Timothy White
Place of Publication: London, UK
Publisher: Elm Tree Books
Year: 1983: **ISBN-10:** 0241109574
Pages: 380: **Price:** £6.95 UK
Description: First UK edition, paperback with color pictorial wrappers, 6" x 9". Note: This comprehensive history of Bob Marley has seen more printings and revisions than any other biography. It covers his life along with some Caribbean history and offers the reader a detailed album list. Illustrated with several black and white photos.

Title: *Catch a Fire: The Life of Bob Marley*
Author: Timothy White
Place of Publication: New York, U.S.
Publisher: Holt, Rinehart & Winston
Year: 1983: **ISBN-10:** 0030635314
Pages: 380: **Price:** $16.95 U.S.
Description: First U.S. edition, hardcover, full black cloth, gilt, in color pictorial wrappers dust jacket, 6.25" x 9.25". Note: This comprehensive history of Bob Marley has seen more printings and revisions than any other biography. It covers his life along with some Caribbean history and offers the reader a detailed album list. Illustrated with several black and white photos. For many years the author donated all royalties generated from this book to Amnesty International.

Title: *Catch a Fire: The Life of Bob Marley*
Author: Timothy White
Place of Publication: New York, U.S.
Publisher: Holt, Rinehart & Winston
Year: 1983: **ISBN-10:** 0030621097
Pages: 380: **Price:** $9.95 U.S.
Description: First U.S. edition, paperback with color pictorial wrappers, 6" x 9". Note: This comprehensive history of Bob Marley has seen more printings and revisions than any other biography. It covers his life along with some Caribbean history and offers the reader a detailed album list. Illustrated with several black and white photos.

Title: *Bob Marley: The Definitive Biography of Reggae's Greatest Star (Illustrated)*
Author: Stephen Davis
Place of Publication: London, UK
Publisher: Panther Books
Year: 1984: **ISBN-10:** 0586061924
Pages: 352: **Price:** £2.95 UK; $6.95 New Zealand; $6.95 Australia
Description: First Panther edition, Second UK printing, paperback with color pictorial wrappers, 4.25" x 7". Note: One of the first in depth biographies about Marley and is illustrated with several black and white photos. It still stands the test of time and has seen many new editions and printings throughout the world. Regarded by many as the best biography written about Bob. Marley.

Title: *Catch a Fire: The Life of Bob Marley*
Author: Timothy White
Place of Publication: London, UK
Publisher: Corgi
Year: 1984: **ISBN-10:** 0552990973
Pages: 412: **Price:** £3.95; $9.95 New Zealand; $8.95 Australia
Description: Second UK edition and printing, first Corgi printing, paperback with color pictorial wrappers, 5" x 7.75". Note: This comprehensive history of Bob Marley has seen more printings and revisions than any other biography. It covers his life along with some Caribbean history and offers the reader a detailed album list. Illustrated with several black and white photos. For many years the author donated all royalties generated from this book to Amnesty International.

Title: *Bob Marley: Reggae King of the World*
Author(s): Malika Lee Whitney and Dermott Hussey (Foreword: Rita Marley)
Place of Publication: Kingston, Jamaica
Publisher: Kingston Publishers Ltd.
Year: 1984: **ISBN:** None Listed
Pages: 207: **Price:** None Listed
Description: First JA edition, hardcover in red library binding, 9" x 12". Note: Contains numerous pictures, discography, tour routes, newspaper clippings and transcripts of interviews. The only located HC copy of this edition is bound in red library binding with white lettering on the spine. It is possibly a fabricoid binding done by a library and not by done by the publisher. Although it looks as if it was published with this binding.

Title: *Bob Marley: Reggae King of the World*
Author(s): Malika Lee Whitney and Dermott Hussey (Foreword: Rita Marley)
Place of Publication: Kingston, Jamaica
Publisher: Kingston Publishers Ltd.
Year: 1984: **ISBN:** None Listed
Pages: 207: **Price:** None Listed
Description: First JA edition, paperback with color pictorial wrappers, 8.75" x 12". Note: A nice picture book and biography from a Jamaican point of view. It contains numerous pictures, discography, tour routes, newspaper clippings and transcripts of interviews. A fantastic book.

Title: *Bob Marley: Reggae King of the World*
Author(s): Malika Lee Whitney and Dermott Hussey (Foreword: Rita Marley)
Place of Publication: New York, U.S.
Publisher: E.P. Dutton
Year: 1984: **ISBN-10:** 0525480889
Pages: 207: **Price:** $14.95 U.S.
Description: First U.S. edition, paperback with color pictorial wrappers, 8.75" x 12". Note: A nice picture book and biography from a Jamaican point of view. It contains numerous pictures, discography, tour routes, newspaper clippings and transcripts of interviews.

Title: *Bob Marley*
Author: Stephen Davis
Place of Publication: Garden City, NY, U.S.
Publisher: Double Day Dolphin
Year: 1985: **ISBN-10:** 0385179561
Pages: 276: **Price:** $9.95 U.S.
Description: First U.S. edition, paperback with color pictorial wrappers, 6" x 9.25". Note: One of the first in depth biographies about Marley and is illustrated with several black and white photos. It still stands the test of time and has seen many new editions and printings throughout the world. Certain libraries have fabricated this edition into a hardcover. Regarded by many as the best biography written about Bob Marley.

Title: *Bob Marley: An Independent Story in Words and Pictures*
Author: Roger St.Pierre
Place of Publication: Essex, UK
Publisher: Anabas
Year: 1985: **ISBN-10:** 1850990085
Pages: 28: **Price:** None Listed
Description: Paperback with color pictorial wrappers, 12" x 12". Note: A short biography and Island Records discography. Illustrated with large color photos. Part of 'The Anabas Look Book Series.'

Title: *Bob Marley: A Bibliography*
Author: National Library of Jamaica
Place of Publication: Kingston, Jamaica
Publisher: National Library of Jamaica
Year: 1985: **ISBN-10:** 9768020016
Pages: 23: **Price:** None Listed
Description: First edition, paperback with printed wrappers, 8.5" x 11". Note: This is a list of materials in the NLJ's collections dealing with Bob Marley. Part of the NLJ's 'Occasional Bibliography Series.' This was the first book of the series. There was a second edition published in 1998.

Title: *Bob Marley*
Author: Chris May (Illustrations by Trevor Parkin)
Place of Publication: London, UK
Publisher: Hamish Hamilton
Year: 1985: **ISBN-10:** 0241114764
Pages: 60: **Price:** £3.95 UK
Description: First printing, hardcover with color pictorial boards, 5.75" x 8.5". Note: A juvenile biography illustrated with black and white drawings by Parkin. Part of Hamish Hamilton's 'Profiles' series.

Title: *The Bob Marley Story*
Author: Madeline Sotheby
Place of Publication: London, UK
Publisher: Hutchinson & Co. (Publishers) Ltd
Year: 1985: **ISBN-10:** 0091600316
Pages: 64: **Price:** None Listed
Description: Paperback with color pictorial wrappers, 5" x 7.5". Note: The Bob Marley story is a short juvenile biography that tells Bob's story from beginning to end. No illustrations. Part of Hutchinson's 'Ace' biography series.

Title: *Catch a Fire: The Life of Bob Marley*
Author: Timothy White
Place of Publication: New York, U.S.
Publisher: Henry Holt & Company
Year: 1986: **ISBN-10:** 0805002405
Pages: 380: **Price:** $9.95 U.S.
Description: Second U.S. edition and printing, paperback with color pictorial wrappers, 6" x 9". Note: PB cites a HC edition with ISBN-10: 0030635314. I don't know if it is a reference to the 1983 HC edition or if there was indeed a new 1986 HC printing using the same 1983 HC ISBN. I have been unable to locate a 1986 HC edition of Catch a Fire. Title page states that this is the fifth printing, revised and updated. Not sure if that is in reference to the two HC and two PB editions published in the UK and U.S. in 1983. If you include the Corgi edition this would be the sixth total printing.

Title: *Bob Marley*
Author: Chris May (Illustrations by Trevor Parkin)
Place of Publication: London, UK
Publisher: Hamish Hamilton
Year: 1987: **ISBN-10:** 0241114764
Pages: 60: **Price:** £3.95 UK
Description: Second printing, hardcover with color pictorial boards, 5.75" x 8.5". Note: A juvenile biography illustrated with black and white drawings by Parkin. Part of Hamish Hamilton's 'Profiles' series.

Title: *Bob Marley*
Author(s): Karen Baggs and Peter Beynon
Place of Publication: Nottingham, UK
Publisher: Newmat
Year: 1988: **ISBN-10:** 187117404x
Pages: 15: **Price:** .45 p UK
Description: Paperback with color pictorial wrappers, 5.75" x 8.25". Note: A very brief juvenile biography illustrated with black and white photos and a short list of albums. Part of Newmat's 'Rock Biographies' series.

Title: *Catch a Fire: The Life of Bob Marley*
Author: Timothy White
Place of Publication: New York, U.S.; Ontario, Canada
Publisher: Henry Holt & Company; Fitzhenry & Whiteside Ltd.
Year: 1989: **ISBN-10:** 0505011528
Pages: 464: **Price:** $12.95 U.S.
Description: Third U.S. printing and edition, paperback with color pictorial wrappers, 6" x 9". Note: This comprehensive history of Bob Marley has seen more printings and revisions than any other biography. It covers his life along with some Caribbean history and offers the reader a detailed album list. Title page states this edition is revised and enlarged. Illustrated with several black and white photos.

Title: Catch a Fire: The Life of Bob Marley
Author: Timothy White
Place of Publication: London, UK
Publisher: Corgi
Year: 1989: **ISBN-10:** 0552990973
Pages: 412: **Price:** None Listed
Description: Second UK edition, third UK printing, second Corgi printing, paperback with color pictorial wrappers, 5" x 7.75". Note: This comprehensive history of Bob Marley has seen more printings and revisions than any other biography. It covers his life along with some Caribbean history and offers the reader a detailed album list. Illustrated with several black and white photos. For many years the author donated all royalties generated from this book to Amnesty International.

Title: *Bob Marley: The Definitive Biography of Reggae's Greatest Superstar (Illustrated)*
Author: Stephen Davis
Place of Publication: London, UK
Publisher: Grafton Books
Year: 1989: **ISBN-10:** 0586061924
Pages: 352: **Price:** £3.99 UK; $15.95 New Zealand; $11.95 Australia
Description: Third UK printing, paperback with color pictorial wrappers, 4.25" x 7". Note: One of the first in depth biographies about Marley and is illustrated with several black and white photos. It still stands the test of time and has seen many new editions and printings throughout the world. Regarded by many as the best biography written about Bob Marley.

Title: *Bob Marley: Reggae King of the World*
Author(s): Malika Lee Whitney and Dermott Hussey (Foreword: Rita Marley)
Place of Publication: London, UK
Publisher: Plexus Publishing Ltd.
Year: 1989 / 1984: **ISBN-10:** 0859650685
Pages: 207: **Price:** £6.95 UK
Description: First UK edition, paperback with color pictorial wrappers, 8.75" x 12". Note: A nice picture book and biography from a Jamaican point of view. It contains numerous pictures, discography, tour routes, newspaper clippings and transcripts of interviews. A hardcover edition was also published by Plexus in 1989 with ISBN-10: 0859650693. May have been published in 1984 not 1989.

Title: *The Philosophy of Bob Marley: Lyrics of his songs, Quotations, Rastafarianism, Songs on Staff Notations for Guitar and Keyboard*
Author: Vitalis Ibeh (Dr.Vitalis Orikeze Ajumbe)
Place of Publication: Owerri, Nigeria
Publisher: Beat On Investments Ltd.
Year: 1990: **ISBN-10:** 9783067486
Pages: 112: **Price:** None Listed
Description: Paperback with color pictorial wrappers. Note: This book was first published in 1990, with revisions in 1995 and 2008. It features lyrics to songs, notable and inspiring quotations and song notation on staff for guitar and keyboards

Title: *Bob Marley*
Author: Stephen Davis
Place of Publications: Rochester, Vt., U.S.
Publisher: Schenkman Books Inc.
Year: 1990: **ISBN-10:** 0870470450
Pages: 286: **Price:** None Listed
Description: Second U.S. edition, hardcover, full red cloth, gilt, 5.75" x 8.75". Note: Revised edition of the 1985 Double Day Dolphin edition. This hardcover edition was printed in limited quantities for libraries. Illustrated with several black and white photos. Regarded by many as the best biography written about Bob Marley.

Title: *Bob Marley*
Author: Stephen Davis
Place of Publications: Rochester, Vt., U.S.
Publisher: Schenkman Books Inc.
Year: 1990: **ISBN-10:** 0870470442
Pages: 286: **Price:** None Listed
Description: Second U.S. edition, paperback with color pictorial wrappers, 5.5" x 8.5". Note: Revised edition of the 1985 Double Day Dolphin edition. Illustrated with several black and white photos. Regarded by many as the best biography written about Bob Marley.

Title: *Joseph: A Rasta Reggae Fable*
Author: Makeda Levi (Barbara Makeda Blake Hannah)
Place of Publication: Kingston, Jamaica
Publisher: Jamaica Media Productions Ltd.
Year: 1991: **ISBN-10:** 9768091118
Pages: 158: **Price:** None Listed
Description: First edition, paperback with color pictorial wrappers, 5.25" x 8". Note: An allegory fable of Joseph, a great reggae musician from Jamaica, who reaches worldwide success and then disappears into the African horizon. Much of it mirrors the life of Bob Marley. A fantastic book.

Title: *Catch a Fire: The Life of Bob Marley*
Author: Timothy White
Place of Publication: London, UK
Publisher: Omnibus Press
Year: 1991: **ISBN-10:** 0711927707
Pages: 476: **Price:** None Listed
Description: Third UK edition, fourth UK printing, paperback with color pictorial wrappers, 6" x 9". Note: This comprehensive history of Bob Marley has seen more printings and revisions than any other biography. It covers his life along with some Caribbean history and offers the reader a detailed album list. Title page states this is the third edition. Illustrated with several black and white photos.

Title: *Catch a Fire: The Life of Bob Marley*
Author: Timothy White
Place of Publication: New York, U.S.; Ontario, Canada
Publisher: Henry Holt & Company; Fitzhenry & Whiteside Limited
Year: 1991: **ISBN-10:** 0805011528
Pages: 476: **Price:** $12.95 U.S.
Description: Third U.S. edition, fourth U.S. printing, paperback with color pictorial wrappers, 6" x 9". Note: This comprehensive history of Bob Marley has seen more printings and revisions than any other biography. It covers his life along with some Caribbean history and offers the reader a detailed album list. Reprint of the 1989 revised and enlarged edition. Illustrated with several black and white photos.

Title: *Catch a Fire: The Life of Bob Marley*
Author: Timothy White
Place of Publication: New York, U.S.; Ontario, Canada
Publisher: Henry Holt; Fitzhenry & Whiteside Limited
Year: 1992: **ISBN-10:** 0805011528
Pages: 476: **Price:** $12.95 U.S.
Description: Third U.S. edition, fifth U.S. printing, paperback with color pictorial wrappers, 6" x 9". Note: This comprehensive history of Bob Marley has seen more printings and revisions than any other biography. It covers his life along with some Caribbean history and offers the reader a detailed album list. Reprint of the 1989 revised and enlarged edition. Illustrated with several black and white photos.

Title: *Joseph: A Rasta Reggae Fable*
Author: Barbara Makeda Blake Hannah (Makeda Levi)
Place of Publication: Kingston, Jamaica
Publisher: Jamaica Media Productions Ltd.
Year: 1992: **ISBN-10:** 9768091118
Pages: 156: **Price:** None Listed
Description: Second edition, paperback with color pictorial wrappers, 5.5" x 8.5". Note: An allegory fable of Joseph, a great reggae musician from Jamaica, who reaches worldwide success and then disappears into the African horizon. Much of it mirrors the life of Bob Marley. Second edition printing receives the inclusion of black and white illustrations by Tekla Ab. A fantastic book.

Title: *Bob Marley: Conquering Lion Of Reggae*
Author: Stephen Davis
Place of Publication: London, UK
Publisher: Plexus Publishing Limited
Year: 1993: **ISBN-10:** 0859651797
Pages: 286: **Price:** £9.99 UK
Description: First Plexus edition, paperback with color pictorial wrappers, 6" x 9". Note: One of the first in depth biographies about Marley and is illustrated with several black and white photos. It still stands the test of time and has seen many new editions and printings throughout the world. New Plexus edition added the subtitle *Conquering Lion of Reggae*. Regarded by many as the best biography written about Bob Marley.

Title: *Bob Marley*
Author: Margaret E. Ward
Place of Publication: Stamford, Conn., U.S.
Publisher: Longmeadow Press
Year: 1993: **ISBN-10:** 0681418664
Pages: 80: **Price:** None Listed
Description: Hardcover, full black cloth, gilt, in color pictorial dust jacket, 9.25" x 12.25". Note: A short juvenile biography about Marley accompanied by many photographs.

Title: *Bob Marley*
Author: Margaret E. Ward
Place of Publication: London, UK
Publisher: Bison Books
Year: 1993: **ISBN-10:** 1858410142
Pages: 73: **Price:** None Listed
Description: Hardcover, full black cloth, gilt, in color pictorial dust jacket, 9.25" x 12.25". Note: A short juvenile biography about Marley accompanied by many photographs.

Title: *Bob Marley: in his own words*
Author: Ian McCann
Place of Publication: London, UK
Publisher: Omnibus Press
Year: 1993: **ISBN-10:** 0711930805
Pages: 96: **Price:** £7.95 UK
Description: First edition, paperback with color pictorial wrappers, 7" x 10". Note: A collection of quotes from Marley on different topics. Illustrated with black and white photos.

Title: *Bob Marley: In His Own Words*
Author: Ian McCann
Place of Publication: London, UK
Publisher: Omnibus Press
Year: 1993: **ISBN-10:** 0711930805
Pages: 96: **Price:** £7.95 UK
Description: Second printing, paperback with color pictorial wrappers, 7" x 10". Note: A collection of quotes from Marley on different topics. Illustrated with black and white photos. This second printing was done within a few years of the first. The only differences I can find between the first two *In His Own Words* are the covers and printing company. The only date listed in this book is 1993.

Title: *Bob Marley (The World's Greatest Composers)*
Author: Marsha Bronson
Place of Publication: Herts, UK
Publisher: Exley Publications Ltd.
Year: 1993: **ISBN-10:** 1850153124
Pages: 64: **Price:** £6.99 UK
Description: Hardcover with color pictorial boards, 6" x 8.5". Note: A more in depth juvenile biography illustrated with color photos. Includes a timeline, recommended albums and glossary. Part of Exley's 'World's Greatest Composers' series.

Title: *Bob Marley: Conquering Lion Of Reggae*
Author: Stephen Davis
Place of Publication: London, UK
Publisher: Plexus Publishing Limited
Year: 1994: **ISBN-10:** 085965222x
Pages: 292: **Price:** £14.99 UK
Description: Second Plexus edition, paperback with color pictorial wrappers, 6" x 9". Note: One of the first in depth biographies about Marley and is illustrated with several black and white photos. It still stands the test of time and has seen many new editions and printings throughout the world. Regarded by many as the best biography written about Bob Marley.

Title: *Bob Marley: Reggae King of the World*
Author(s): Malika Lee Whitney and Dermott Hussey (Foreword: Rita Marley)
Place of Publication: Rohnert Park, Calif., U.S.
Publisher: Pomegranate Artbooks
Year: 1994: **ISBN-10:** 156640987x
Pages: 207: **Price:** $16.95 U.S.
Description: Second U.S. printing, paperback with color pictorial wrappers, 8.75" x 12". Note: A nice picture book and biography from a Jamaican point of view. It contains transcripts of interviews, pictures, discography, tour routes, newspaper clippings and several pictures.

Title: *Marley: The Illustrated Legend 1945-1981*
Author: Barry Lazell
Place of Publication: London, UK
Publisher: Hamlyn
Year: 1994: **ISBN-10:** 0600582213
Pages: 80: **Price:** None Listed
Description: First printing, paperback with color pictorial wrappers, 9" x 11.5". Note: A short biography accompanied by many photographs including a few rare ones.

Title: *Bob Marley*
Author: Chris Welch
Place of Publication: London, UK
Publisher: Carlton
Year: 1994: **ISBN-10:** 1858680573
Pages: 120: **Price:** None Listed
Description: First printing, paperback with color pictorial wrappers, 5.75" x 5". Note: A short biography illustrated with color photos. Includes a section on Chris Blackwell and a pretty extensive discography. One of the first CD sized books.

Title: *Marley and me: The Real Story as told to Mike Henry*
Author(s): Don Taylor with Mike Henry
Place of Publication: Kingston, Jamaica
Publisher: Kingston Publishers
Year: 1994: **ISBN-10:** 1885642016
Pages: 266: **Price:** None Listed
Description: First JA printing, paperback with color pictorial wrappers, 5.5" x 8.5". Note: The autobiography of Don Taylor, one time manager of Bob Marley. Illustrated with black and white photos.

Title: *Catch a Fire: The Life of Bob Marley*
Author: Timothy White
Place of Publication: New York, U.S.; Ontario, Canada
Publisher: Henry Holt; Fitzhenry & Whiteside Limited
Year: 1994: **ISBN-10:** 080511528
Pages: 476: **Price:** $13.95 U.S.
Description: Third U.S. edition, sixth U.S. printing, paperback with color pictorial wrappers, 6" x 9". Note: This comprehensive history of Bob Marley has seen more printings and revisions than any other biography. It covers his life along with some Caribbean history and offers the reader a detailed album list. Reprint of the 1989 revised and enlarged edition. Illustrated with several black and white photos.

Title: *Bob Marley: songs of freedom*
Author(s): Adrian Boot and Chris Salewicz (Executive editor: Rita Marley)
Place of Publication: New York, U.S.
Publisher: Viking Penguin
Year: 1995: **ISBN-10:** 067085784x
Pages: 288: **Price:** $29.95 U.S. until April 30, 1995 $34.95 U.S. thereafter
Description: First U.S. edition, hardcover, full black cloth, gilt, in color pictorial dust jacket, 10.5" x 10.5". Note: This book contains lots of vivid photographs as well as informative text. Released in conjunction with Island's four album box set of the same name. The authorized biography on Bob Marley.

Title: *Bob Marley: songs of freedom*
Author(s): Adrian Boot and Chris Salewicz (Executive editor: Rita Marley)
Place of Publication: London, UK
Publisher: Bloomsbury Publisher Plc
Year: 1995: **ISBN-10:** 074751853x
Pages: 288: **Price:** £25.00 UK
Description: First U.K. edition, hardcover, full black cloth, gilt, in color pictorial dust jacket, 10.5" x 10.5". Note: This book contains lots of vivid photographs as well as informative text. Released in conjunction with Island's four album box set of the same name. The authorized biography of Bob Marley.

Title: *Bob Marley: songs of freedom*
Author(s): Adrian Boot and Chris Salewicz (Executive editor: Rita Marley)
Place of Publication: London, UK
Publisher: Bloomsbury Publisher Plc
Year: 1995: **ISBN-10:** 0747523568
Pages: 288: **Price:** £14.99 UK
Description: First UK edition, paperback with color pictorial wrappers, 10.25" x 10.25". Note: This book contains lots of vivid photographs and informative text. Released in conjunction with Island's four album box set of the same name. The authorized biography of Bob Marley.

Title: *So Much Things To Say: My Life as Bob Marley's Manager*
Author(s): Don Taylor with Mike Henry
Place of Publication: London, UK
Publisher: Blake Publishing Ltd.
Year: 1995: **ISBN-10:** 185782119x
Pages: 262: **Price:** None Listed
Description: First UK edition, hardcover, dark blue library binding, no lettering, in color pictorial dust jacket, 6" x 9". Note: The autobiography of Don Taylor, one time manager of Bob Marley. Illustrated with black and white photos.

Title: *Marley and Me: The Real Bob Marley Story Told By His Manager Don Taylor*
Author(s): Don Taylor with Mike Henry
Place of Publication: New York, U.S.
Publisher: Barricade Books
Year: 1995: **ISBN-10:** 1569800448
Pages: 256: **Price:** $14.95 U.S.
Description: First U.S. edition, paperback with color pictorial wrappers, 6" x 9". Note: The autobiography of Don Taylor, one time manager of Bob Marley. Illustrated with black and white photos.

Title: *Bob Marley: They Died Too Young*
Author: Millie Gilfoyle
Place of Publication: Bristol, UK
Publisher: Paragon Books
Year: 1995: **ISBN-10:** 0752511157
Pages: 74: **Price:** None Listed
Description: Hardcover, color pictorial boards in color pictorial dust jacket, 3.25" x 4.5". Note: Packaged in a small pocket sized book, this is a short biography illustrated with color photos. Part of the 'They Died Too Young' series.

Title: *Marley: The Illustrated Legend 1945-1981*
Author: Barry Lazell
Place of Publication: London, UK
Publisher: Hamlyn
Year: 1995: **ISBN-10:** 0600582213
Pages: 80: **Price:** £9.99 UK
Description: Second printing, paperback with color pictorial wrappers, 9" x 11.5". Note: A short biography accompanied by many photographs including a few rare ones.

Title: *Bob Marley*
Author: Chris Welch
Place of Publication: London, UK
Publisher: Carlton Books
Year: 1996: **ISBN-10:** 1858680573
Pages: 120: **Price:** None Listed
Description: Second printing, paperback with color pictorial wrappers, 5.75" x 5". Note: A short biography illustrated with color photos. Includes a section on Chris Blackwell and a pretty extensive discography.

Title: *Bob Marley: An intimate portrait by his mother*
Author: Cedella Booker with Anthony Winkler
Place of Publication: London, UK
Publisher: Viking
Year: 1996: **ISBN-10:** 0670869910
Pages: 250: **Price:** £17.00 UK
Description: First UK edition, hardcover, full black cloth, lettered in green, in color pictorial dust jacket, 6.25" x 9.5". Note: The autobiography of Bob's mother, Cedella Marley-Booker, and her personal accounts of Bob's life. Includes details about his agonizing final days in Germany. Illustrated with personal family photos.

Title: *Catch a Fire: The Life of Bob Marley*
Author: Timothy White
Place of Publication: New York, U.S.; Ontario, Canada
Publisher: Henry Holt / Owl; Fitzhenry & Whiteside Ltd.
Year: 1996: **ISBN-10:** 080511528
Pages: 476: **Price:** $14.95 U.S.; $20.95 Canada
Description: Third U.S. edition, seventh U.S. printing, paperback with color pictorial wrappers, 6" x 9". Note: This comprehensive history of Bob Marley has seen more printings and revisions than any other biography. It covers his life along with some Caribbean history and offers the reader a detailed album list. Reprint of the 1989 revised and enlarged edition. Illustrated with several black and white photos.

Title: *Bob Marley: An intimate portrait by his mother*
Author(s): Cedella Booker with Anthony Winkler
Place of Publication: London, UK
Publisher: Penguin Books
Year: 1997: **ISBN-10:** 0140258140
Pages: 250: **Price:** £7.99 UK; $17.95 Australia
Description: First UK edition, Paperback in color pictorial wrappers, 5.25" x 7.75". Note: The autobiography of Bob's mother, Cedella Marley-Booker, and her personal accounts of Bob's life. Includes details about his agonizing final days in Germany. Illustrated with personal family photos.

Title: *Bob Marley*
Author: Scotty Bennett- introduction
Place of Publication: London, UK
Publisher: Virgin Publishing Ltd.
Year: 1997: **ISBN-10:** 1852276932
Pages: 93: **Price:** None Listed
Description: Hardcover, color pictorial boards, 5" x 5.75". Note: A short juvenile biography illustrated with color photos. Includes a nice timeline and short bios about several people who were important in Marley's life. Part of the 'Modern Icons' series.

Title: *Bob Marley*
Author: Scotty Bennett- introduction
Place of Publication: New York, U.S.
Publisher: St. Martin's Press
Year: 1997: **ISBN-10:** 0312179375
Pages: 93: **Price:** $9.95 U.S.
Description: Hardcover, color pictorial boards in color pictorial dust jacket, 5" x 7.5". Note: A short juvenile biography illustrated with color photos. Includes a nice timeline and short bios about several people who were important in Marley's life. Part of the 'Modern Icons' series.

Title: *Bob Marley*
Author: Sean Dolan
Place of Publication: Philadelphia, U.S.
Publisher: Chelsea House Publishers
Year: 1997: **ISBN-10:** 079102041x
Pages: 120: **Price:** None Listed
Description: First edition, hardcover, color pictorial boards, 7.5" x 9.5". Note: A juvenile biography illustrated with black and white photos. Includes a timeline, bibliography and select discography. Part of the 'Black Americans of Achievement' series.

Title: *Bob Marley*
Author: Sean Dolan
Place of Publication: Philadelphia, U.S.
Publisher: Chelsea House Publishers
Year: 1997: **ISBN-10:** 0791032558
Pages: 120: **Price:** $8.95 U.S.
Description: First edition, paperback with color pictorial wrappers, 7" x 9.25". Note: A juvenile biography illustrated with black and white photos. Includes a timeline, bibliography and select discography. Part of the 'Black Americans of Achievement' series.

Title: *Bob Marley: Songs of Freedom*
Author(s): Adrian Boot and Chris Salewicz (Executive editor: Rita Marley)
Place of Publication: New York, U.S.
Publisher: Viking Penguin Studio
Year: 1998: **ISBN-10:** 0140241131
Pages: 288: **Price:** $19.95 U.S.
Description: Paperback with color pictorial wrappers, 10" x 10.25". Note: First U.S. paperback edition. This book contains lots of vivid photographs as well as informative text. A fantastic photo / biography book. The authorized biography of Bob Marley.

Title: *Catch a Fire: The Life of Bob Marley*
Author: Timothy White
Place of Publication: New York, U.S.; Ontario, Canada
Publisher: Henry Holt / Owl; Fitzhenry & Whiteside Ltd.
Year: 1998: **ISBN-10:** 050506009x
Pages: 476: **Price:** $14.95 U.S.; $20.95 Canada
Description: Fourth U.S. edition, eighth U.S. printing, paperback with color pictorial wrappers, 6" x 9". Note: This comprehensive history of Bob Marley has seen more printings and revisions than any other biography. It covers his life along with some Caribbean history and offers the reader a detailed album list. Illustrated with several black and white photos.

Title: *Bob Marley: Reggae King of the World*
Author(s): Malika Lee Whitney and Dermott Hussey (Foreword: Rita Marley)
Place of Publication: Rohnert Park, Calif., U.S.
Publisher: Pomegranate Communications
Year: 1998: **ISBN-10:** 156640987x
Pages: 207: **Price:** $17.95 U.S.
Description: Third U.S. printing, paperback with color pictorial wrappers, 8.75" x 12". Note: A nice picture book and biography from a Jamaican point of view. It contains numerous pictures, discography, tour routes, newspaper clippings and transcripts of interviews.

Title: *Bob Marley: Island Prophet*
Author: Mitchell Uscher
Place of Publication: Kansas City, U.S.
Publisher: Andrews McMeel Publishing
Year: 1999: **ISBN-10:** 0740700561
Pages: 79: **Price:** $4.95 U.S.; $6.95 Canada
Description: Hardcover, black pictorial boards, lettered in red, in color pictorial dust jacket, 3.25" x 4". Note: A pocket sized biography illustrated with color photos. Includes a brief year by year account of his recording and touring schedules along with quotes from Marley.

Title: *Bob Marley: They Died Too Young*
Author: Millie Gilfoyle
Place of Publication: Philadelphia, U.S.
Publisher: Chelsea House Publishers
Year: 1999: **ISBN-10:** 0791052281
Pages: 48: **Price:** None Listed
Description: Second edition, hardcover, color pictorial boards, 6.25" x 9.25". Note: Released the second time in a much larger format, this is a brief biography illustrated with color photos. Part of the 'They Died Too Young' series.

Title: *Catch a Fire: The Life of Bob Marley*
Author: Timothy White
Place of Publication: New York, U.S.
Publisher: Henry Holt & Company
Year: 2000: **ISBN-10:** 050506009x
Pages: 556: **Price:** $17.00 U.S.; $24.95 Canada
Description: Fourth U.S. edition, ninth U.S. printing, paperback with color pictorial wrappers, 6" x 9". Note: This comprehensive history of Bob Marley has seen more printings and revisions than any other biography. It covers his life along with some Caribbean history and offers the reader a detailed album list. Reprint of the 1998 new revised and enlarged edition. Illustrated with several black and white photos.

Title: *Catch a Fire: The Life of Bob Marley*
Author: Timothy White
Place of Publication: London, UK
Publisher: Omnibus Press
Year: 2000: **ISBN-10:** 0711983909
Pages: 554: **Price:** £14.95 UK
Description: Fourth UK edition, fifth UK printing, paperback with color pictorial wrappers, 6" x 9". Note: This comprehensive history of Bob Marley has seen more printings and revisions than any other biography. It covers his life along with some Caribbean history and offers the reader a detailed album list. Illustrated with several black and white photos. Title pages states "this edition published 2000". It also cites three copyright dates; 1983, 1998 and 2000. Omnibus never published the 1998 edition as they had plenty of stock of the previous edition.

Title: *Bob Marley: Reggae King of The World*
Author(s): Malika Lee Whitney and Dermott Hussey (Foreword: Rita Marley)
Place of Publication: Kingston, Jamaica
Publisher: LMH Publishing Ltd.
Year: 2001: **ISBN-10:** 976625060x
Pages: 184: **Price:** [?]
Description: Sixth total printing, second JA printing, paperback with color pictorial wrappers, 8.75" x 12". Note: A nice picture book and biography from a Jamaican point of view. It contains numerous pictures, discography, tour routes, newspaper clippings and transcripts of interviews.

Title: *Marley and me: The Real Story as Told to Mike Henry*
Author(s): Don Taylor with Mike Henry
Place of Publication: Kingston, Jamaica
Publisher: LMH Publishing Ltd.
Year: 2001: **ISBN-10:** 9768184027
Pages: 226: **Price:** None Listed
Description: Second JA printing, paperback with color pictorial wrappers, 5.5" x 8.5". Note: The autobiography of Don Taylor, one time manager of Bob Marley. Illustrated with black and white photos.

Title: *56 Thoughts From 56 Hope Road: The Sayings & Psalms of Bob Marley*
Author(s): Cedella Marley, Gerald Hausman and Bob Marley
Place of Publication: Miami, U.S.
Publisher: Tuff Gong Books
Year: 2002: **ISBN-10:** 0971975809
Pages: 82: **Price:** None Listed
Description: Paperback with color pictorial wrappers, 3.75" x 4.25". Note: 56 sayings and Psalms of Marley's selected by the authors. A selection of quotes and song lyrics. Cedella Marley is one of Bob's daughters.

Title: *Bob Marley & Peter Tosh-Get Up! Stand Up!: Diary of a Reggaeophile*
Author: Fikisha Cumbo (Foreword by Roberta Flack)
Place of Publication: Brooklyn, U.S.
Publisher: Case International
Year: 2002: **ISBN-10:** 0972445706
Pages: 322: **Price:** $24.95 U.S.
Description: Paperback with color pictorial wrappers, 8.5" x 11". Note: A personal account of the relationships the author had with both Marley and Tosh. Includes numerous fantastic photos of both legends taken by Cumbo.

Title: *Bob Marley, My Son*
Author(s): Cedella Marley Booker with Anthony C. Winkler
Place of Publication: Lanham, Md., U.S.
Publisher: Taylor Trade Publishing
Year: 2003: **ISBN-10:** 0878332987
Pages: 250: **Price:** $22.95 U.S.
Description: Reprint, First U.S. printing, hardcover, red quarter board and yellow boards, lettered in black, in color pictorial dust jacket, 6.25" x 9.25". Note: Reprint of Viking / Penguin UK edition. The autobiography of Marley's mother, Cedella Marley Booker, and her personal accounts of Bob's life. Includes details about his agonizing final days in Germany. Illustrated with personal family photos.

Title: *Guns and Ganja: The Secret Life of Bob Marley*
Author(s): Don Taylor with Mike Henry
Place of Publication: London, UK
Publisher: John Blake Publishing Ltd.
Year: 2003: **ISBN-10:** 1857825969
Pages: 258: **Price:** £7.99 UK
Description: Fourth edition, paperback with color pictorial wrappers, 5" x 7.75". Note: Fourth printing of Don Taylor's story with a few minor changes to the text. Illustrated with black and white photos.

Title: *One Love: Life with Bob Marley and The Wailers, Words and Photographs by Lee Jaffe, Introduction and Interviews by Roger Steffens*
Author(s): Lee Jaffe (Words and Photographs) and Roger Steffens (Introduction and Interview)
Place of Publication: New York, U.S.; London, UK
Publisher: W.W. Norton
Year: 2003: **ISBN-10:** 0393051439
Pages: 224: **Price:** $40.00 U.S.; $58.00 Canada
Description: Hardcover, red quarter cloth and black cloth, lettered in black, in color pictorial dust jacket, 10.25" x 11.75". Note: Could also be classified as a photo book. The firsthand account of Jaffe's friendship with Marley and living with him in Jamaica. Illustrated with his photos of Bob and others including Karl Pitterson. Interviews by Steffens.

Title: *One Love: Life with Bob Marley and The Wailers, Words and Photographs by Lee Jaffe, Introduction and Interviews by Roger Steffens*
Author(s): Lee Jaffe (Words and Photographs) and Roger Steffens (Introduction and Interview)
Place of Publication: New York, U.S.; London, UK
Publisher: W.W. Norton
Year: 2003: **ISBN-10:** 0393323684
Pages: 224: **Price:** $25.00 U.S.; $36.00 Canada
Description: Paperback with color pictorial wrappers, 10" x 11.5". Note: Could also be classified as a photo book. The firsthand account of Jaffe's friendship with Bob and living with him in Jamaica. Illustrated with his photos of Bob and others including Karl Pitterson. Interviews by Steffens.

Title: *Bob Marley: "Talking"*
Author: Ian McCann
Place of Publication: London, UK
Publisher: Omnibus Press
Year: 2003: **ISBN-10:** 0711997667
Pages: 112: **Price:** $14.95 U.S.
Description: Second edition, paperback with color pictorial wrappers, 6.25" x 9.25". Note: New title for the *In His Own Words* book. A collection of quotes from Marley on different topics. Illustrated with black and white photos.

Title: *Bob Marley: The Man & His Music*
Author(s): Eleanor Wint and Carolyn Cooper editors
Place of Publication: Kingston, Jamaica
Publisher: Arawak Publications
Year: 2003: **ISBN-10:** 9769504793
Pages: 112: **Price:** None Listed
Description: Paperback with color pictorial wrappers, 6" x 9". Note: A collection of essays from the 1995 symposium held in Jamaica to celebrate the 50th anniversary of Marley's birth.

Title: *Reggae Rebel: The Life of Peter Tosh*
Author: Chris Salewicz
Place of Publication: London, UK
Publisher: Omnibus Press
Year: 2003: **ISBN-10:** 0711988706
Pages: 272: **Price:** N/A
Description: Paperback with color pictorial wrappers, 6" x 9". Note: This book was never written or published. John Masouri is currently authoring a Peter Tosh biography which will be published by Omnibus Press in 2010 and may use the same title. Tosh was an original Wailer along with Marley and Bunny Wailer. He ventured out on a successful solo career in 1974. He was murdered in his Jamaican home in 1987. Like his childhood friend Bob Marley, Peter Tosh too is considered a Legend.

Title: *No Woman No Cry: My Life with Bob Marley (Advanced uncorrected proofs)*
Author(s): Rita Marley with Hettie Jones
Place of Publication: New York, U.S.
Publisher: Hyperion
Year: 2003: **ISBN-10:** 0786868678
Pages: 224: **Price:** $22.95 U.S.; $33.95 Canada
Description: Paperback with printed wrappers, 6.25" x 9.25". Note: Advanced copy with highlights issued on Dec 22, 2003.

Back cover of advanced copy

Title: *The Bob Marley Reader: Every Little Thing Gonna Be Alright*
Author(s): Hank Bordowitz editor (Foreword by Roger Steffens)
Place of Publication: Cambridge, Mass., U.S.
Publisher: Da Capo Press
Year: 2004: **ISBN-10:** 0306813408
Pages: 314: **Price:** $17.95 U.S.; $27.95 Canada
Description: Paperback with color pictorial wrappers, 6" x 9". Note: A collection of articles written about Marley by some of the most notable reggae journalist of our time.

Title: *No Woman No Cry: My Life with Bob Marley*
Author(s): Rita Marley with Hettie Jones
Place of Publication: New York, U.S.
Publisher: Hyperion
Year: 2004: **ISBN-10:** 0786868678
Pages: 209: **Price:** $22.95 U.S.; $33.95 Canada
Description: First U.S. edition, hardcover, black quarter cloth and grey boards, lettered in silver, in color pictorial dust jacket, 6.5" x 9.5". Note: Marley's wife describes her relationship with him from beginning to end and her own life as a musician and business woman. Illustrated with personal photos.

Marketing cover for *No Woman No Cry*

Title: *No Woman No Cry: My Life with Bob Marley*
Author(s): Rita Marley with Hettie Jones:
Place of Publication: London, UK
Publisher: Sidgwick & Jackson
Year: 2004: **ISBN-10:** 0283073640
Pages: 209: **Price:** None Listed
Description: First UK HC edition, hardcover, full black cloth, gilt, in color pictorial dust jacket, 6.25" x 9.5". Note: Marley's wife describes her relationship with him from beginning to end and her own life as a musician and business woman. Illustrated with personal photos.

Title: *No Woman No Cry: My Life with Bob Marley*
Author(s): Rita Marley with Hettie Jones:
Place of Publication: London, UK
Publisher: Sidgwick & Jackson
Year: 2004: **ISBN-10:** 0283070080
Pages: 209: **Price:** [?]
Description: First UK PB edition, paperback with color pictorial wrappers, 6" x 9". Note: Marley's wife describes her relationship with him from beginning to end and her own life as a musician and business woman. Illustrated with personal photos.

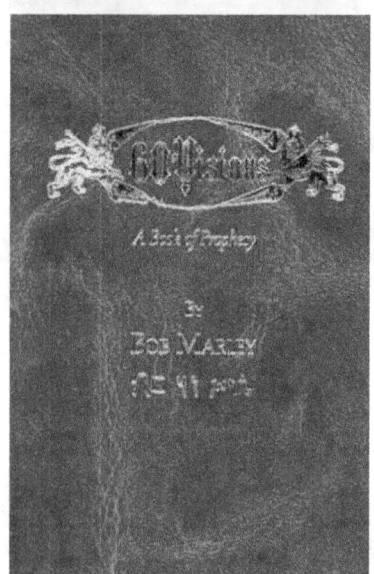

Title: *60 Visions: A Book of Prophesy by Bob Marley*
Author(s): Cedella Marley and Bob Marley
Place of Publication: Miami, U.S.
Publisher: Tuff Gong Books
Year: 2004: **ISBN-10:** 0971975817
Pages: 98: **Price:** None Listed
Description: Soft cover in imitation leather, 4" x 5.75". Note: 60 of Marley's most eloquent quotes selected by his daughter.

Title: *No Woman No Cry: My Life With Bob Marley*
Author(s): Rita Marley with Hettie Jones
Place of Publication: London, UK
Publisher: Pan Books
Year: 2005: **ISBN-10:** 0330493302
Pages: 209: **Price:** £7.99 UK
Description: Second UK edition, paperback with color pictorial wrappers, 5.25" x 7.75". Note: Marley's wife describes her relationship with him from beginning to end and her own life as a musician and business woman. Illustrated with personal photos.

Title: *No Woman No Cry: My Life With Bob Marley*
Author(s): Rita Marley with Hettie Jones
Place of Publication: New York, U.S.
Publisher: Hyperion
Year: 2005: **ISBN-10:** 0786887559
Pages: 209: **Price:** $14.95 U.S.; $21.95 Canada
Description: First U.S. PB edition, paperback with color pictorial wrappers, 5.5" x 8". Note: Marley's wife describes her relationship with him from beginning to end and her own life as a musician and business woman. Illustrated with personal photos.

Title: *Catch a Fire: The Life of Bob Marley*
Author: Timothy White
Place of Publication: New York, U.S.
Publisher: Owl / Henry Holt & Company
Year: 2006: **ISBN-10:** 0805080864
Pages: 556: **Price:** $17.00 U.S.; $22.95 Canada
Description: Fifth U.S. edition, tenth U.S. printing, paperback with color pictorial wrappers, 6" x 9". Note: This comprehensive history of Bob Marley has seen more printings and revisions than any other biography. It covers his life along with some Caribbean history and offers the reader a detailed album list. Illustrated with several black and white photos. Last U.S. edition to date with additional text by White's widow Judy Garlan.

Title: *Catch a Fire: The Life of Bob Marley*
Author: Timothy White
Place of Publication: London, UK
Publisher: Omnibus Press
Year: 2006: **ISBN-10:** 1846091578
Pages: 600: **Price:** £ 16.95 UK
Description: Fifth UK edition, sixth UK printing, paperback with color pictorial wrappers, 6" x 9". Note: This comprehensive history of Bob Marley has seen more printings and revisions than any other biography. It covers his life along with some Caribbean history and offers the reader a detailed album list. Illustrated with several black and white photos. Last UK edition to date with additional text by White's widow Judy Garlan. The UK edition of this book continues to sell about 3000 copies a year.

Title: *The Book of Exodus: The Making & Meaning of Bob Marley & The Wailers Album Of The Century*
Author: Vivien Goldman
Place of Publication: New York, U.S.
Publisher: Three Rivers Press
Year: 2006: **ISBN-10:** 1400052866
Pages: 326: **Price:** $14.95 U.S.; $21.00 Canada
Description: Paperback with color pictorial wrappers, 5.5" x 8.5". Note: Documents Marley and The Wailers time after the assassination attempt on his life in December 1976. Includes a firsthand account of the *Exodus* recording sessions in London and the ensuing tour. A detail packed book. Illustrated with black and white photos including a rare one of Bob with the One Love Peace Concert Committee members. There were two different marketing covers used. Had a second printing in 2007.

Title: *Before The Legend: The Rise of Bob Marley*
Author: Christopher John Farley
Place of Publication: New York, U.S.
Publisher: Amistad
Year: 2006: **ISBN-10:** 0060539917
Pages: 216: **Price:** $21.95 U.S.; $28.50 Canada
Description: Hardcover, black quarter boards and tan boards, gilt, in color pictorial dust jacket, 5.75" x 8.5". Note: A fresh detailed look at Marley's life before the international fame and stardom. In-depth research by the author turns up new information which had never been reported previously. Tells his story from birth through the release of *Catch a Fire* in 1973.

Title: *Marley Legend: An Illustrated Life of Bob Marley*
Author: James Henke
Place of Publication: San Francisco, U.S.
Publisher: Chronicle Books
Year: 2006: **ISBN-10:** 0811850366
Pages: 64: **Price:** $35.00 U.S.
Description: Hardcover, color pictorial boards issued with color cardboard slip case, 10" x 11". Note: Fully illustrated biography with removable memorabilia reproductions including Marley's notebook, handwritten lyrics and concert memorabilia. Comes with an interview CD.

Colored cardboard slip case for Marley Legend

Title: *Joseph: A Rasta Reggae Fable*
Author: Barbara Makeda Blake Hannah
Place of Publication: Oxford, UK
Publisher: Macmillilan Education
Year: 2006: **ISBN-10:** 140506143x
Pages: 202: **Price:** None Listed
Description: Third edition, paperback with color pictorial wrappers, 5.5" x 8.5". Note: An allegory fable of Joseph, a great reggae musician from Jamaica, who reaches worldwide success and then disappears into the African horizon. Much of it mirrors the life of Bob Marley. A fantastic book.

Title: *Bob Marley: Conquering Lion of Reggae*
Author: Stephen Davis
Place of Publication: London, UK
Publisher: Plexus Publishing Limited
Year: 2006: **ISBN-10:** 085965222x
Pages: 292: **Price:** £14.99 UK
Description: Paperback with color pictorial wrappers, 6" x 9". Note: First reprint of second Plexus revised edition. One of the first in depth biographies about Marley and is illustrated with several black and white photos. It still stands the test of time and has seen many new editions and printings throughout the world. Regarded by many as the best biography written about Bob Marley.

Title: *Bob Marley: Black Americans of Achievement*
Author: Sherry Beck Paprocki
Place of Publication: New York, U.S.
Publisher: Chelsea House Publishers
Year: 2006: **ISBN-10:** 0791092135
Pages: 111: **Price:** None Listed
Description: Second edition, hardcover, color pictorial boards, 6.75" x 9.5". Note: Second edition to Sean Dolan's book of the same title. Updates include a section on Marley's 2005 60th birthday celebrations in Addis Ababa, Ethiopia. Illustrated with color photos. Part of the 'Black Americans of Achievement Legacy Edition.'

Title: *Exodus: Bob Marley & The Wailers Exodus Exile 1977 30th Anniversary*
Author: Richard Williams
Place of Publication: London, UK
Publisher: Weidenfeld & Nicholson / The Orion Publisher Group
Year: 2007: **ISBN-13:** 9780297853220
Pages: 144: **Price:** £25.00 UK
Description: Hardcover, full red boards, gilt, in color pictorial dust jacket, 9.75" x 9.75". Note: Released in conjunction with the 30th anniversary of the *Exodus* album, several contributing writers tell the story of *Exodus*. It is illustrated with several color and black and white photos and comes with the original album on CD.

Title: *Bob Marley: Herald of the Postcolonial World?*
Author: Jason Toynbee
Place of Publication: Cambridge, UK and Malden, Mass., U.S.
Publisher: Polity Press
Year: 2007: **ISBN-13:** 9780745630885
Pages: 263: **Price:** None Listed
Description: Hardcover, color pictorial boards, 6" x 9". Note: An academic look at Marley's rise to be the first third world superstar and social contributor. The author traces Marley's start in the ghetto through his rise to the world stage as well as his lasting impact.

Title: *Bob Marley: Herald of the Postcolonial World?*
Author: Jason Toynbee
Place of Publication: Cambridge, UK and Malden, Mass., U.S.
Publisher: Polity Press
Year: 2007: **ISBN-10:** 9780745630892
Pages: 263: **Price:** None Listed
Description: Paperback with color pictorial wrappers, 5.5" x 8.25". Note: An academic look at Marley's rise to be the first third world superstar and social contributor. The author traces Marley's start in the ghetto through his rise to the world stage as well as his lasting impact.

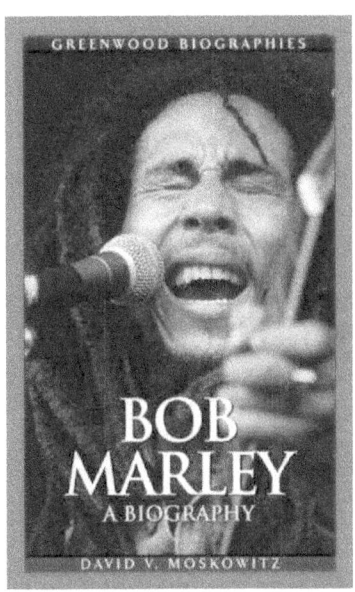

Title: *Bob Marley: A Biography*
Author: David V. Moskowitz
Place of Publication: Westport, Conn., U.S.
Publisher: Greenwood Press
Year: 2007: **ISBN-13:** 9780313338793
Pages: 125: **Price:** None Listed
Description: Hardcover, color pictorial boards, 6.5" x 9.5". Note: A succinct and accurate biography about the life of Bob Marley.

Title: *The Words & Music of Bob Marley*
Author: David Moskowitz
Place of Publication: Westport, Conn., U.S.
Publisher: Praeger Publishers
Year: 2007: **ISBN-10:** 0275989356
Pages: 177: **Price:** None Listed
Description: Hardcover, full black cloth, lettered in silver, in color pictorial dust jacket, 6.25" x 9.5". Note: A chronological look at Marley's musical output with biographical information inserted when necessary. Illustrated with black and white photos. Part of the 'Praeger Singer-Songwriter Collection.'

Title: *Before The Legend: The Rise of Bob Marley*
Author: Christopher John Farley
Place of Publication: New York, U.S.
Publisher: Amistad
Year: 2007: **ISBN-13:** 9780060539924
Pages: 217: **Price:** $9.95 U.S.; $12.50 Canada
Description: Paperback with color pictorial wrappers, 5.25" x 8". Note: A fresh detailed look at Marley's life before the international fame and stardom. In-depth research by the author turns up new information which had never been reported previously. Tells his story from birth through the release of *Catch a Fire* in 1973.

Title: *Bob Marley and the Wailers: Pop Rock, Popular Rock Superstars of Yesterday and Today*
Author: Rosa Waters
Place of Publication: Broomall, Pa., U.S.
Publisher: Mason Crest Publishers
Year: 2008: **ISBN-13:** 9781422201923
Pages: 64: **Price:** None Listed
Description: Hardcover, color pictorial boards, 7.5" x 9.5". Note: A juvenile biography illustrated with color photos. Includes a select discography, list of accomplishments and awards and a chronology of events in Marley's life. Part of the 'Pop Rock' series.

Title: *Bob Marley and the Wailers: Pop Rock, Popular Rock Superstars of Yesterday and Today*
Author: Rosa Waters
Place of Publication: Broomall, Pa., U.S.
Publisher: Mason Crest Publishers
Year: 2008: **ISBN-13:** 9781422203170
Pages: 64: **Price:** $7.95 U.S.
Description: Paperback with color pictorial wrappers, 5.5" x 8". Note: A juvenile biography illustrated with color photos. Includes a select discography, list of accomplishments and awards and a chronology of events in Marley's life. Part of the 'Pop Rock' series.

Title: *Bob Marley: Conquering Lion of Reggae*
Author: Stephen Davis
Place of Publication: London, UK
Publisher: Plexus Publishing Limited
Year: 2008: **ISBN-10:** 085965222x
Pages: 328: **Price:** £14.99 UK
Description: Paperback with color pictorial wrappers, 6" x 9". Note: Second printing of revised Plexus edition. One of the first in depth biographies about Marley and is illustrated with several black and white photos. Regarded by many as the best biography written about Bob Marley. I have not been able to locate a 2008 printing of this book but have seen several advertised and when ordered, the 2006 edition always shows up. The Plexus website lists a 328 page edition but lacks information such as the year it was published.

Title: *Wailing Blues: The Story of Bob Marley's Wailers*
Author: John Masouri
Place of Publication: London, UK
Publisher: Omnibus Press
Year: 2008: **ISBN-13:** 9781846096891
Pages: 582: **Price:** £19.95 UK; $29.99 U.S.
Description: Hardcover, full black cloth, gilt, in color pictorial dust jacket, 6.5" x 9.5". Note: The story of Bob's Wailers in particular bass player and musical arranger, Aston "Family Man / Fams" Barrett and his brother and Wailers drummer Carly. This insightful book offers a firsthand account of life in the studio and on the road with Marley and Family Man's failed court case against the Marley Estate and Island Records. Fams is regarded by many as one of the all-time greatest bass players.

Title: *Bob Marley*
Author: Garry Steckles
Place of Publication: Oxford, UK
Publisher: Macmillan Caribbean and Signal Books Ltd.
Year: 2008: **ISBN-13:** 978140508143: Macmillan; 9781904955412: Signal
Pages: 267: **Price:** None Listed
Description: Paperback with color pictorial wrappers, 4.75" x 7". Note: Dual publishers, Macmillan covers the Caribbean market, Signal covers the UK market. A concise and succinct biography about Marley that traces his life from beginning to end as well as his lasting impact. Presents the Estate battles in an easy to follow manner. Part of the 'Caribbean Lives' series.

Title: *Bob Marley: A Life*
Author: Garry Steckles
Place of Publication: Northampton, Mass., U.S.
Publisher: Interlink Books
Year: 2008: **ISBN-13:** 9781566567336
Pages: 212: **Price:** $17.00 U.S.
Description: Paperback with color pictorial wrappers, 6" x 9". Note: Same text as 'Caribbean Lives' series. Interlink published this book for the U.S. market.

Title: *Reggae Poet: the story of Bob Marley*
Author: Calvin Craig Miller
Place of Publication: Greensboro, N.C., U.S.
Publisher: Morgan Reynolds Publishing.
Year: 2008: **ISBN-10:** 1599350718
Pages: 128: **Price:** None Listed
Description: Hardcover, color pictorial boards, 6.25" x 9.25". Note: A juvenile biography that includes several color and black and white photos. Part of the 'Modern Music Masters' series.

Title: *Marley*
Author(s): Luke Crampton, Dafydd Rees and Wellesley Marsh
Place of Publication: Koln, Germany
Publisher: Taschen GmbH
Year: 2009: **ISBN-13:** #1: 9783836511285, #2: 9783836511292
Pages: 192: **Price:** None Listed
Description: Color pictorial flexi-binding, 5.75" x 7.75". Note: Released in two editions each containing three different languages: #1: English, German and French; #2: Italian, Portuguese and Spanish. A very concise and accurate biography about Marley and is loaded with vivid color photos. Part of Taschen's 'Music Icons' series. A unique book.

Title: *Marley Journal*
Author: Lowell Taubman MD
Place of Publication: U.S.
Publisher: LuLu.com
Year: 2009: **ISBN-13:** 9780578018775
Pages: 494: **Price:** $34.78 U.S.
Description: Paperback with color pictorial wrappers, 4.25" x 6.75". Note: There have been three editions. The book is an archivist's musings on trading, negotiating and life. Marley related vignettes with a philosophical and humorous edge. Marley Blog is written as a puzzle, and Marley III is in a traditional format. The author is a Wailers lover and collector and regularly blogs about Marley and life.

Title: *Bob Marley: The Untold Story*
Author: Chris Salewicz
Place of Publication: London, UK
Publisher: Harper Collins Entertainment
Year: 2009: **ISBN-10:** 0007255527
Pages: 427: **Price:** £20.00 UK; $55.00 U.S.
Description: Hardcover, 6" x 9". Note: A detailed examination of the life of Bob Marley by a veteran journalist and reggae author.

Title: *Bob Marley: The Untold Story*
Author: Chris Salewicz
Place of Publication: London, UK
Publisher: Harper Collins Entertainment
Year: 2009: **ISBN-10:** 0007255543
Pages: 427: **Price:** £12.99 UK; $32.99 U.S.
Description: Paperback with color pictorial wrapping, 6" x 9". Note: A detailed examination of the life of Bob Marley by a veteran journalist and reggae author.

Additional Biographies

Title: *Bob Marley and the Wailers*: **Author(s):** Jonathan Green and Adrian Boot-photographs: **Place of Publication:** London, UK: **Publisher:** Wise: **Year:** 1977: **ISBN-10:** [?]: **Pages:** 87: **Price:** [?]: **Description:** Note: May be a music book.

Title: *Bob Marley: Rasta Vision of a new world*: **Author:** Sebastian Clarke: **Place of Publication:** Canada: **Publisher:** Book Society of Canada: **Year:** 1983 **ISBN-13:** 9780435821609: **Pages:** [?]: **Price:** [?]: **Description:** [?]

Title: *Bob Marley Remembered*: **Author(s):** Jim Aldred and Liidia Heuff: **Place of Publication:** Richmond Hill, Ontario, Canada: **Publisher:** Printers Devil Press: **Year:** 1984: **ISBN-10:** 0969105134: **Pages:** 8: **Price:** [?]: **Description:** (Note: 300 copies printed)

Title: *Bob Marley: Rasta Visions New World*: **Author:** Suzanne Clarke: **Place of Publication:** UK: **Publisher:** Gower Publisher Ltd.: **Year:** 1986: **ISBN-10:** 0566009080: **Pages:** [?]: **Price:** [?]: **Description:** Hardcover. Note: Have no confirmation that this book exist and/or its relation to Sebastian Clarke's book of a similar title. ISBN searches come up with this book.

Title: *Rock Lives: Bob Marley*: **Author:** Chris Salewicz: **Place of Publication:** UK: **Publisher:** Orion Publisher Group: **Year:** 1998: **ISBN-10:** 0752812319: **Pages:** [?]: **Price:** £ 16.99 UK: **Description:** Hardcover

Title: *Bob Marley A Bibliography (occasional bibliography series no.3)*: **Author(s):** National Library of Jamaica, Compiled by Winsome Edwards, Edited by Byron Palmer: **Place of Publication:** Kingston, Jamaica: **Publisher:** National Library of Jamaica: **Year:** 1998: **ISBN-10:** 976802032: **Pages:** 21: **Price:** None Listed: **Description:** Second edition, Paperback with printed wrappers.

Title: *Bob Marley: A Musical Drama*: **Author:** James Irungu: **Place of Publication:** Nairobi: **Publisher:** [?]: **Year:** 2000: **ISBN:** [?]: **Pages:** 60: **Price:** [?]: **Description:** [?

Discographies and Song Guides

Many books claim to be a discography but a true discography is more than just a list of records with their labels and date of release. A true discography must include the following information: vocalist, musicians and their instruments, name on the label, label numbers, country of release, producer, engineer, number of tracks on the master tape, studio and lastly the matrix number in the wax of the record. The only true discography that conforms to those academic requirements is the *Definitive Discography* by Roger Steffens and Leroy Jodie Pierson. The rest of the books in this chapter are classified as album or song guides, which is not a bad thing as many of them offer a quick review or guide to the numerous Bob Marley and The Wailers releases. Some publications, such as *Lyrical Genius* by Kwame Dawes, present an in-depth analysis of Bob's music and lyrics.

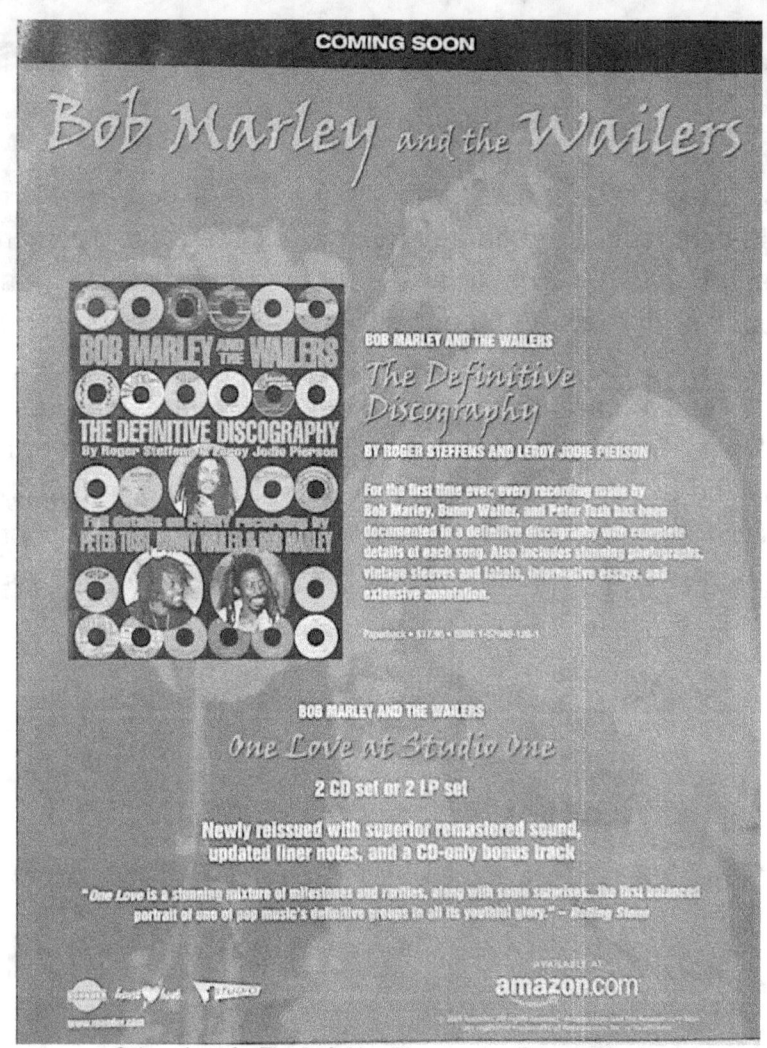

Color advert for The Definitive Discography, Rounder Books
The Beat Magazine Vol. 24 #5 2005 7.25" x 9.75"

Title: *Bob Marley: The Illustrated Disco / Biography*
Author: Observer Station
Place of Publication: London, UK
Publisher: Omnibus Press
Year: 1985: **ISBN-10:** 0711906157
Pages: 96: **Price:** None Listed
Description: Paperback with color pictorial wrappers, 7.75" x 4.75". Note: An early discography of Marley albums and singles. Quite nice for the time period. Illustrated with black and white photos of album covers and 7" labels.

Title: *The Complete Guide to the Music of Bob Marley*
Author: Ian McCann
Place of Publication: London, UK
Publisher: Omnibus Press
Year: 1994: **ISBN-10:** 0711935505
Pages: 130: **Price:** $7.95 U.S.
Description: Paperback with color pictorial wrappers, 5.5" x 5". Note: An insightful and helpful guide to several of the officially released Marley albums. This book is often times sold with an interview disc and slip case as seen below. Illustrated with black and white album covers.

Cardboard slip case that accompanies the Complete Guide when packaged with the interview picture disc.

Title: *Bob Marley: Soul Survivor- The Stories Behind Every Song*
Author: Maureen Sheridan
Place of Publication: Kent, UK
Publisher: Seven Oaks
Year: 1999: **ISBN-10:** 1862000506
Pages: 148: **Price:** None Listed
Description: Hardcover, color pictorial boards in color pictorial dust jacket, 9" x 11.25". Note: Stories and background information to several Bob Marley and The Wailers songs. Illustrated with black and white and color photos.

Additional cover shown with Chris Welch as author and *The Wailing Soul* as the title. This book was never published with Welch's name as author or associated with it.

Title: *Soul Rebel: The Stories Behind every Bob Marley Song 1962-1981*
Author: Maureen Sheridan
Place of Publication: New York, U.S.
Publisher: Thunder Mouth Press
Year: 1999: **ISBN-10:** 1560252049
Pages: 144: **Price:** $22.95 U.S.
Description: Paperback with color pictorial wrappers, 8.5" x 11". Note: Stories and background information to several Bob Marley and The Wailers songs. Illustrated with black and white and color photos.

Title: *The Wailing Soul: The Stories Behind Every Bob Marley Song 1962-1981*
Author: Maureen Sheridan
Place of Publication: London, UK
Publisher: Carlton Books Ltd.
Year: 1999: **ISBN-10:** 1858687497
Pages: 144: **Price:** [?]
Description: Paperback with color pictorial wrappers, 8.75" x 11". Note: Stories and background information to several Bob Marley and The Wailers songs. Illustrated with black and white and color photos.

Title: *L'integrale: Les Secrets De Toutes Ses Chansons Bob Marley 1962-1981*
Author: Maureen Sheridan
Place of Publication: Paris, France
Publisher: Presses De La Cite
Year: 2001: **ISBN-10:** 2258051185
Pages: 144: **Price:** 22,70 €
Description: Paperback with color pictorial wrappers, 8.75" x 11". Note: French edition of *Soul Rebel*. Stories and background information to several Bob Marley and The Wailers songs. Illustrated with black and white and color photos.

Title: *Bob Marley: Songs of African Redemption*
Author: Adebayo Ojo
Place of Publication: Lagos State, Nigeria
Publisher: Malthouse Press Ltd.
Year: 2000: **ISBN-10:** 9780231188
Pages: 169: **Price:** None Listed
Description: Paperback with color pictorial wrappers, 8.5" x 5.75". Note: A serious appraisal of the meaning and purpose of Marley's songs as well as their interpretations.

Title: *The Metaphysical Interpretation of Bob Marley's Exodus*
Author: Issachar Ye Amlak
Place of Publication: St Croix, USVI
Publisher: The Rise
Year: 2002: **ISBN-10:** 0972302905
Pages: 52: **Price:** $14.95 U.S.
Description: Paperback with color pictorial wrappers, 8.5" x11". Note: An intellectual examination of the songs from the *Exodus* album. Illustrated with black and white photos.

Title: *Bob Marley: Lyrical Genius*
Author: Kwame Dawes
Place of Publication: London, UK
Publisher: Sanctuary Publishing Ltd.
Year: 2002: **ISBN-10:** 1860744338
Pages: 356: **Price:** £12.99 UK; $18.95 U.S.
Description: First edition, paperback with color pictorial wrappers, 5.25" x 8.5". Note: Marley's lyrics are dissected and assessed in the context that they were written as well as evaluating their enduring merit in the world of political poetry. This book gives some insight into Bob's meaningful lyrics.

Title: *Bob Marley: Der Ausnahmepoet*
Author: Kwame Dawes
Place of Publication: Bergkirchen, Germany
Publisher: PPV Medien
Year: 2004: **ISBN-10:** 3932275888
Pages: 384: **Price:** [?]
Description: Paperback with color pictorial wrappers, 5.25" x 8.25". Note: German edition of *Lyrical Genius*. Marley's lyrics are dissected and assessed in the context that they were written as well as evaluating their enduring merit in the world of political poetry. This book gives some much needed insight into Bob's meaningful lyrics.

Title: *Bob Marley: Story und Songs kompakt*
Author(s): Ian McCann and Harry Hawke
Place of Publication: Berlin, Germany
Publisher: Bosworth
Year: 2004: **ISBN-10:** 3936026920
Pages: 208: **Price:** [?]
Description: Paperback with color pictorial wrappers, 4.25" x 6.75". Note: German edition of *Bob Marley: The Complete Guide to His M*usic. An insightful and helpful guide to several of the officially released Marley albums. Additional cover shown. Illustrated with black and white album covers.

Title: *Bob Marley: the Complete Guide to his Music*
Author(s): Ian McCann and Harry Hawke
Place of Publication: London, UK
Publisher: Omnibus Press
Year: 2004: **ISBN-10:** 0711998841
Pages: 144: **Price:** $6.95 U.S.
Description: Paperback with color pictorial wrappers, 4.25" x 7". Note: An insightful and helpful guide to several of the officially released Marley albums. Illustrated with black and white album covers.

Title: *Bob Marley: The Complete Guide To The Music Of Bob Marley*
Author(s): Ian McCann and Harry Hawke
Place of Publication: London, UK
Publisher: Omnibus Press
Year: 2004: **ISBN-10:** 0711998841
Pages: 144: **Price:** [?]
Description: Paperback with color pictorial wrappers, 4.5" x 7". Note: This was a working title and cover that was never published or used.

Title: *Bob Marley and The Wailers: The Definitive Discography (Full Details on Every Recording by Peter Tosh, Bunny Wailer & Bob Marley)*
Author(s): Roger Steffens and Leroy Jodie Pierson
Place of Publication: Cambridge, Mass., U.S.
Publisher: Rounder Books
Year: 2005: **ISBN-10:** 1579401201
Pages: 177: **Price:** $17.95 U.S.; $22.95 Canada
Description: Paperback with color pictorial wrappers, 8.5" x 11". Note: Complete discography of every song recorded by Marley, Tosh and Wailer. Includes all information required of a true discography in addition to a 12 page color photo section of gorgeous 7" labels. Includes extensive biographical information on subjects and authors. Illustrated with black and white photos of memorabilia and album covers. An invaluable book. Book design and layout by Geoff Gans.

Marketing placard used before release of the Definitive Discography. Included for interest purposes only.

Title: *Bob Marley and the Wailers: The Definitive Discography*
Author(s): Roger Steffens and Leroy Jodie Pierson
Place of Publication: Kingston, Jamaica
Publisher: LMH Publishing Ltd.
Year: 2005: **ISBN-10:** 9768184752
Pages: 177: **Price:** None Listed
Description: Paperback with color pictorial wrappers, 8.5" x 11". Note: Complete discography of every song recorded by Marley, Tosh and Wailer. Includes all information required of a true discography in addition to a 12 page color photo section of gorgeous 7" labels. Includes extensive biographical information on subject and authors. Illustrated with black and white photos of memorabilia and album covers. An invaluable book. Book design and layout by Geoff Gans. A must for any Wailers fan and worth every penny of the $17.95 price tag.

Title: *Bob Marley: His Musical Legacy*
Author: Jeremy Collingwood
Place of Publication: London, UK
Publisher: Cassell Illustrated
Year: 2005: **ISBN-10:** 1844033430
Pages: 192: **Price:** £25.00 UK
Description: Hardcover, red, gold and green boards, lettered in black, in color pictorial dust jacket, 9.75" x 11.25". Note: A collector's guide to the original singles released by Marley, including release dates and label information. Includes information about tour dates, promo posters and collecting. Illustrated with color photos of Marley and memorabilia. A very well put together and enjoyable book.

His musical legacy shown with red, gold and green boards.

Title: *Dictionnaire des chansons de Bob Marley*
Author: Elodie Maillot
Place of Publication: Nantes, France
Publisher: Editions de Tournon
Year: 2005: **ISBN-10:** 2914237367
Pages: 316: **Price:** [?]
Description: Paperback with color pictorial wrappers, 6" x 9.5". Note: Marley's songs explained with the stories behind them as well as the biography of his life and explanations of Rastafari.

Title: *l'integrale Bob Marley: les secrets de toutes ses chansons*
Author: Maureen Sheridan
Place of Publication: Paris, France
Publisher: Hors Collection Editions
Year: 2005: **ISBN-10:** 2258065887
Pages: 190: **Price:** 15 €
Description: Paperback with color pictorial wrappers, 5.5" x 9". Note: 2005 French edition of Sheridan's *Soul Rebel* book. Stories and background information to several Bob Marley and The Wailers songs. No illustrations.

Title: *Bob Marley: His Musical Legacy*
Author: Jeremy Collingwood
Place of Publication: Hildesheim-Zurich, Switzerland
Publisher: Edition Olms Zurich
Year: 2005: **ISBN-10:** 3283005060
Pages: 191: **Price:** [?]
Description: Hardcover, red, gold and green boards, lettered in black, in color pictorial dust jacket, 9.75" x 11.25". Note: Swiss edition of *His Musical Legacy*. A collector's guide to the original singles released by Marley, including release dates and label information. Includes information about tour dates, promo posters and collecting. Illustrated with color photos of Marley and memorabilia.

Title: *Bob Marley: His Musical Legacy*
Author: Jeremy Collingwood
Place of Publication: London, UK
Publisher: Cassell Illustrated
Year: 2006: **ISBN-10:** 1844035050
Pages: 192: **Price:** £16.99 UK
Description: Paperback with color pictorial wrappers, 9.5" x 11". Note: A collector's guide to the original singles released by Marley, including release dates and label information. Includes information about tour dates, promo posters and collecting. Illustrated with color photos of Marley and memorabilia. A very well put together and enjoyable book.

Early paperback cover for *His Musical Legacy* that was never used.

Title: *Bob Marley*
Author: Jeremy Collingwood
Place of Publication: Milan, Italy
Publisher: Giunti
Year: 2006: **ISBN-10:** 8809049330
Pages: 192: **Price:** 19,50 €
Description: Hardcover, red, gold and green boards, lettered in black, in color pictorial dust jacket, 9.75" x 11.25". Note: Italian edition of *His Musical Legacy*. A collector's guide to the original singles released by Marley, including release dates and label information. Also includes information about tour dates, promo posters and collecting.

Title: *Bob Marley: Su Legado Musical*
Author: Jeremy Collingwood
Place of Publication: Barcelona, Spain
Publisher: Blume
Year: 2006: **ISBN-13:** 9788498010978
Pages: 192: **Price:** 29,90 €
Description: Hardcover, red, gold and green boards, lettered in black, in color pictorial dust jacket, 9.75" x 11.25". Note: Spanish edition of *His Musical Legacy*. A collector's guide to the original singles released by Marley, including release dates and label information. Also includes information about tour dates, promo posters and collecting. Illustrated with color photos of Marley and memorabilia.

Title: *Bob Marley: The Complete Guide to His Music*
Author(s): Ian McCann, Harry Hawke and Ooishi Hazime (Translation: Okamoto Tiaki)
Place of Publication: Japan
Publisher: Shinko Music Publishing Co.
Year: 2006: **ISBN-10:** 4401630238
Pages: 313: **Price:** ¥1,785
Description: Paperback with color pictorial wrappers, 5" x 7.25". Note: Japanese edition of *Bob Marley: The Complete Guide to His Music*. An insightful and helpful guide to several of the officially released Marley albums. An alternate cover is shown in the Japan biography section.

Title: *Guia musical de Bob Marley*
Author: Ian McCann
Place of Publication: Colonia del Valle, Mexico
Publisher:: Grupo Editorial Tomo
Year: 2008: **ISBN-10:** 9706663576
Pages: 204: **Price:** $114.00 Peso
Description: Paperback with color pictorial wrappers. Note: Spanish edition of *The Complete Guide to the Music of Bob Marley*. An insightful and helpful guide to several of the officially released Marley albums.

Title: *Bob Marley: Lyrical Genius*
Author: Kwame Dawes
Place of Publication: London, UK
Publisher: Bobcat Books
Year: 2008: **ISBN-13:** 100825673526
Pages: 356: **Price:** $17.95 U.S.
Description: Second edition, paperback with color pictorial wrappers, 5.25" x 8.25". Note: Marley's lyrics are dissected and assessed in the context they were written and evaluating their enduring merit in the world of political poetry. This book gives some insight into Marley's meaningful lyrics.

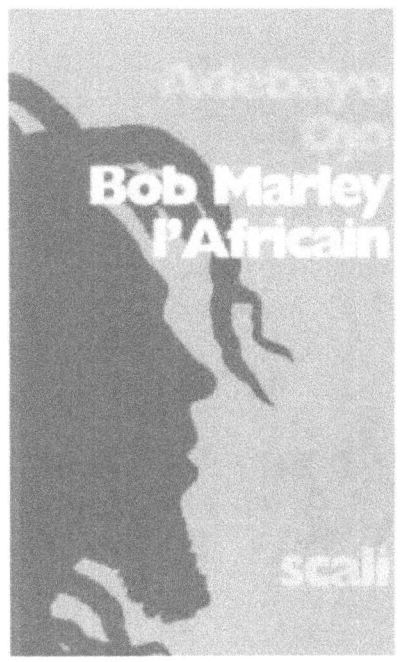

Title: *Bob Marley: l'Africain*
Author(s): Adebayo Ojo (Translation: Bruno Blum and Tao Delhaye)
Place of Publication: Paris, France
Publisher: Scali
Year: 2008: **ISBN-10:** 2350122557
Pages: 320: **Price:** 24 €
Description: Paperback with color pictorial wrapper, 5.5" x 8.75". Note: French edition of the Ojo's *Songs of African Redemption*.

Color promo poster for Bob Marley: Songs of Freedom, Viking Studio Books 1995
16.5" x 23.25"

Photography Books

It has been said that at one time Bob Marley was the most photographed person on earth. Millions of photos have been taken of him and thousands have been compiled into fabulous photography books. The images in these books are a delight for any reader. Fans can anticipate that new material in this category will continue to be published for years to come. There are several photographers out there, such as Kim Gottlieb-Walker and Jeff Cathrow, who have taken countless photos of Bob but have yet to publish a book of their images. Let's hope that one day their fabulous photos will see a proper release. Every book in this chapter is filled with photos of Bob or contains photos of Marley memorabilia, album covers or other reggae runnings. Some books include vivid photos with simple text while others, such as *Rebel Music* by Kate Simon, could be considered works of art. There are several books in this section which could be considered a photo book and biography wrapped into one package. Some of these books posed a problem to me as to where to include them in this bibliography, such as *One Love* by Lee Jaffe and Roger Steffens. For the most part, those books that are heavier on information than photography will be found in the biography section.

#

Color advert for Bob Marley: Spirit Dancer, W.W. Norton The Beat Vol. 13 #5 1994 3.5" x 9.75"

Black and white advert for One Love and Spirit Dancer, W.W. Norton The Beat Vol. 22 #6 2003 3.5" x 9.75"

Title: *Bob Marley: Soul Rebel - Natural Mystic*
Author(s): Vivien Goldman and Adrian Boot
Place of Publication: London, UK
Publisher: Hutchinson Publishing Group Ltd. / Eel Pie
Year: 1981: **ISBN-10:** (0)091464811
Pages: 96: **Price:** £2.95 UK
Description: First printing, paperback with color pictorial wrappers, 8.25" x 11.5". Note: A brief Marley biography by Goldman accompanied by some of Boot's iconic photos of Bob. A very nice early biography and photo book. The ISBN printed on the book only contains 9 numbers. This book was also issued with the limited edition Island Records Nine LP box set.

Title: *Bob Marley: Soul Rebel - Natural Mystic*
Author(s): Vivien Goldman and Adrian Boot
Place of Publication: New York, U.S.
Publisher: St. Martin's Press
Year: 1982: **ISBN-10:** 0312087276
Pages: 96: **Price:** $6.95 U.S.
Description: Second printing, paperback with color pictorial wrappers, 8.25" x 10.5". Note: A brief Marley biography by Goldman accompanied by some of Boot's iconic photos of Bob. A very nice early biography and picture book.

Title: *Bob Marley: Rebel with a Cause-a Photographic Record of the Visions and the Message of the King of Reggae from Natty Dread to Exodus*
Author: Dennis Morris
Place of Publication: London, UK
Publisher: Epoch Productions
Year: 1986: **ISBN:** None Listed
Pages: 58: **Price:** None Listed
Description: First edition, paperback with color pictorial wrappers, 11.5" x 11.5". Note: A sample of Morris' Marley photos.

Title: *Bob Marley: Rebel with a Cause-a Photographic Record of the Visions and the Message of the King of Reggae from Natty Dread to Exodus*
Author: Dennis Morris
Place of Publication: London, UK
Publisher: D.M.M.P.
Year: 1991: **ISBN:** None Listed
Pages: 58: **Price:** None Listed
Description: Second edition, paperback with color pictorial wrappers, 11.5" x 11.5". Note: A sample of Morris' photos of Marley. Book was issued with Trojan four-CD box set *The Early Years 1969-1973*. This book was also published by Omnibus Press with title *Reggae Rebel*.

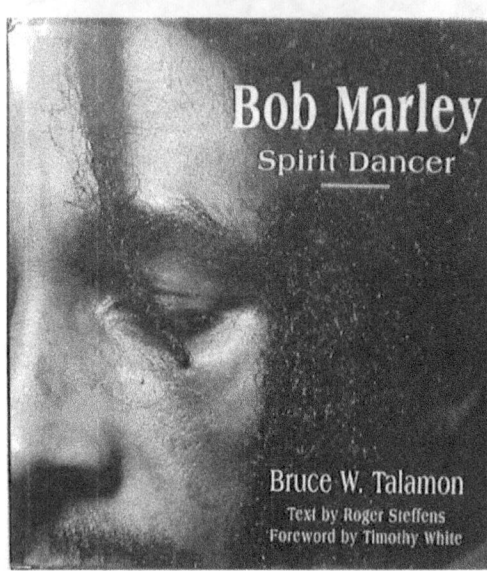

Title: *Bob Marley: Spirit Dancer*
Author(s): Bruce W. Talamon with text by Roger Steffens (Foreword by Timothy White)
Place of Publication: New York, U.S. and London, UK
Publisher: W.W. Norton
Year: 1994: **ISBN-10:** 0393036863
Pages: 128: **Price:** $35.00 U.S.; $45.00 Canada
Description: Hardcover, full black cloth, lettered in silver, in color pictorial dust jacket, 10.25" x 11.5". Note: 83 of Talamon's black and white photographs of Marley both on and off stage. Also included is detailed biographical text by Steffens.

Title: *Bob Marley: Spirit Dancer*
Author(s): Bruce W. Talamon with text by Roger Steffens (Foreword by Timothy White)
Place of Publication: New York, U.S. and London, UK
Publisher: W.W. Norton
Year: 1994: **ISBN-10:** 0393312003
Pages: 128: **Price:** $17.95 U.S.; $22.99 Canada
Description: Paperback with color pictorial wrappers, 10" x 11". Note: 83 of Talamon's black and white photographs of Marley both on and off stage. Also included is detailed biographical text by Steffens.

Title: *Bob Marley: Spirit Dancer*
Author(s): Bruce W. Talamon, with text by Roger Steffens (Foreword by Timothy White)
Place of Publication: Munich, Germany
Publisher: Schirmer / Mosel
Year: 1995: **ISBN-10:** 3888147816
Pages: 128: **Price:** None Listed
Description: Hardcover, black boards, lettered in red, in color pictorial dust jacket, 10.5" x 11.25". Note: German edition of *Spirit Dancer*. 83 of Talamon's black and white photographs of Marley both on and off stage. Also included is detailed biographical text by Steffens.

Title: *Bob Marley: A Book of Post Cards*
Author: N/A
Place of Publication: Rohnert Park, Calif., U.S.
Publisher: Pomegranate
Year: 1996: **ISBN-10:** 0876543689
Pages: 30: **Price:** $9.95 U.S.
Description: Paperback with color pictorial wrappers, 4.75" x 7". Note: As the title states, a collection of 30 postcards that can be framed, mailed or kept in the book.

Title: *Bob Marley: A tear out photo book*
Author: Toby Ingham
Place of Publication: London, UK
Publisher: Oliver Books
Year: 1997: **ISBN-10:** 1870049357
Pages: 40: **Price:** None Listed
Description: Paperback with color pictorial wrappers, 9" x 11.5". Note: Brief text with 20 tear-out color photos suitable for framing.

Title: *A Rasta's Pilgrimage: Ethiopian Faces and Places*
Author: Neville Garrick
Place of Publication: Rohnert Park, Calif., U.S.
Publisher: Pomegranate
Year: 1998: **ISBN-10:** 0764908944
Pages: 128: **Price:** $25.00 U.S.
Description: Paperback with color pictorial wrappers, 12" x 8.75". Note: A visual journey through Ethiopia from the capital to the country. Neville Garrick was Bob's art director hence the inclusion. This is the only book in this bibliography that does not feature Marley.

Title: *Stir It Up: reggae album cover art*
Author: Chris Morrow
Place of Publication: San Francisco, U.S.
Publisher: Chronicle Books
Year: 1999: **ISBN-10:** 0811826163
Pages: 120: **Price:** $24.95 U.S.
Description: Paperback with color pictorial wrappers, 10.5" x 10.5". Note: Bunny Wailer pictured on the cover of this U.S. edition. Contains lots of info about Marley album art and reggae cover art in general. Bunny is the last living original Wailer. Like Tosh, he too went solo in 1974. His first album *Blackheart Man* is a roots reggae masterpiece. He continues to record and tour occasionally. Most of the time he lives a quiet life in Jamaica.

Title: *Reggae: une musique, un art: les plus belles pochettes d' alibrary bindingums*
Author: Chris Morrow
Place of Publication: France
Publisher: Alternatives
Year: 1999: **ISBN-10:** 2862271918
Pages: 120: **Price:** 29,73 €
Description: Paperback with color pictorial wrappers, 10.5" x 10.5". Note: French edition of *Stir It Up*. Contains lots of info about Marley album art and reggae cover art in general.

Title: *Bob Marley: a rebel life-A photobiography*
Author(s): Bruno Blum and Dennis Morris
Place of Publication: London, UK
Publisher: Plexus Publishing Limited
Year: 1999: **ISBN-10:** 0859652688
Pages: 128: **Price:** £14.99 UK; $19.95 U.S.
Description: First edition, paperback with color pictorial wrappers, 9.25" x 11.5". Note: Containing 150 of Morris' photos and text by Bruno Blum, this is a visual treat for all Marley fans. Bruno Blum is an un-credited author.

Title: *Couleur reggae*
Author: Bruno Blum
Place of Publication: Paris, France
Publisher: Tana
Year: 2001: **ISBN-10:** 2845670478
Pages: 8 pages of text with 20 loose glossy photos: **Price:** 22 €
Description: Hardcover, color pictorial boards, 12" x 14". Note: Text by Blum as well as 20 large glossy black and white loose photographs suitable for framing.

Title: *Color reggae*
Author: Bruno Blum (Translation: Giovanna Elisa Taibi)
Place of Publication: Italy
Publisher: L'ippocampo
Year: 2001: **ISBN-10:** 8888585109
Pages: 8 pages of text with 20 loose glossy photos: **Price:** None Listed
Description: Hardcover, color pictorial boards, 12" x 14". Note: Italian edition of *Couleur Reggae*. Text by Blum as well as 20 large glossy black and white loose photographs suitable for framing.

Title: *The World of Reggae Featuring Bob Marley: Treasures from Roger Steffens' Reggae Archives*
Author: Roger Steffens
Place of Publication: Beverly Hills, Calif., U.S.
Publisher: Global Treasures
Year: 2001: **ISBN-10:** 0970791305
Pages: 96: **Price:** $25.00 U.S.; $40.00 overseas
Description: Paperback with color pictorial wrappers, 11" x 11". Note: Hundreds of LP and memorabilia photos with a great Marley section. This book was released in conjunction with Roger's year long + exhibit of his reggae memorabilia on the Queen Mary ocean liner in Long Beach, California. Features rare Selassie and Marley memorabilia. Book design by Geoff Gans of Culver City. A visual delight.

Title: *Rebel Music Bob Marley & Roots Reggae*
Author(s): Kate Simon (text by 24 contributors)
Place of Publication: Surrey, UK
Publisher: Genesis Publications Ltd.
Year: 2004: **ISBN-10:** 1399473799
Pages: 256: **Price:** £495.00 UK-Deluxe Edition
Description: Hardcover, full dark brown leather binding, gilt, cover lettered in white, green, red and yellow. Issued in wooden box as shown, 10" x 14.5". Note: 2000 copies produced, 350 of which were deluxe editions. Book contains hundreds of Kate's fantastic photos and intriguing text about Marley by 24 contributing writers. Deluxe edition is signed by Simon and Eric Clapton. Photo comes from the Genesis website at www.genesis-publications.com.

Title: *Rebel Music Bob Marley & Roots Reggae*
Author(s): Kate Simon (text by 24 contributors)
Place of Publication: Surrey, UK
Publisher: Genesis Publications Ltd.
Year: 2004: **ISBN-10:** 1399473799
Pages: 256: **Price:** £250.00 UK-Regular Edition
Description: Hardcover, brown quarter leather binding and light brown cloth, gilt, cover label lettered in white, green, red and yellow. Issued in wooden slip case, 10" x 14.5". Note: 2000 copies produced, 1650 of which were regular editions. Book contains hundreds of Kate's fantastic photos and intriguing text about Marley by 24 contributing writers. Regular edition is signed by Simon. This book is a true piece of art that is a visual treat in many ways. There may be a paperback edition published one day.

Wooden slip case issued with the regular edition of Kate Simon's *Rebel Music*.

Title: *Bob Marley: a rebel life-A photobiography*
Author(s): Bruno Blum and Dennis Morris
Place of Publication: London, UK
Publisher: Plexus Publishing Limited
Year: 2003: **ISBN-10:** 0859653315
Pages: 128: **Price:** £14.99 UK; $19.95 U.S.
Description: Second edition, paperback with color pictorial wrappers, 9.25" x 11.5". Note: Containing 150 of Morris' photos and text by Bruno Blum, this is a visual treat for all Marley fans. Bruno Blum is an un-credited author.

Title: *Bob Marley: Spirit Dancer*
Author(s): Bruce W. Talamon with text by Roger Steffens (Foreword by Timothy White)
Place of Publication: New York, U.S. and London, UK
Publisher: W.W. Norton
Year: 2003: **ISBN-10:** 0393321738
Pages: 160: **Price:** $13.00 U.S.; $19.50 Canada
Description: Second edition, paperback with color pictorial wrappers, 5" x 5.75". Note: 83 of Talamon's black and white photographs of Bob both on and off stage. Also includes detailed biographical text by Steffens. This second edition was released in a CD sized format.

Title: *Bob Marley: un rebelle un sage-une photobiographie*
Author(s): Bruno Blum and Dennis Morris
Place of Publication: Paris, France
Publisher: Tana
Year: 2006: **ISBN-10:** 2845673248
Pages: 150: **Price:** 20 €
Description: Paperback with color pictorial wrappers, 9.25" x 11.5". Note: French edition of *a rebel life*. Containing 150 of Morris' photos and text by Bruno Blum, this is a visual treat for all Marley fans. Bruno Blum is an un-credited author.

Title: *Bob Marley: Icon*
Author: Dennis Morris
Place of Publication: Japan
Publisher: Excite
Year: 2006: **ISBN-10:** 4903396045
Pages: 134: **Price:** ¥ 3,800
Description: Hardcover, full brown boards, lettered in green, in color pictorial dust jacket, 8.5" x 12". Note: Photos of Marley that Morris took throughout his career. Published in conjunction with a Japanese exhibit of Dennis' photos. Originally issued in a limited edition cardboard box with a t-shirt and other promotional items.

Title: Visual Music: First Ever Photographs of *Bob Marley*
Author: David Brooks
Place of Publication: London, UK
Publisher: David Brooks Publisher
Year: [?]: **ISBN-10:** 0955261902
Pages: 56: **Price:** [?]
Description: Hardcover, 8.2" x 11.7". Note: The story through text and photographs of how Brooks came to accompany Marley on his final tour in 1980. As of printing this book has yet to be published. There may be a change in publishers.

Title: *Roger Steffens & Peter Simon's Reggae Scrapbook*
Author: Roger Steffens and Peter Simon (Foreword by Toots Hibbert, Introduction by Stephen Davis)
Place of Publication: San Rafael, Calif., U.S.
Publisher: Insight Editions
Year: 2007: **ISBN-10:** 1933784237
Pages: 160: **Price:** $45.00 U.S.; $57.00 Canada; £30.00 UK
Description: Hardcover, full brown pictorial boards, lettered in white, in color pictorial dust jacket, 11.25" x 10.25". Note: A fascinating dive into the world of reggae. Includes color photos, interesting interviews from the genres most important figures and is full of removable memorabilia items. A treat for reggae loving eyes.

Image of Bob shown on back board of Roger and Peter's Reggae Scrapbook.

Title: *Bob Marley: Soul Rebel- ein fotografisches Portrat*
Author(s): David Burnett (Translation: Thorsten Wortman)
Place of Publication: Berlin, Germany
Publisher: Schwarzkopf & Schwarzkopf
Year: 2009: **ISBN-10:** 3896028731
Pages: 176: **Price:** 49,90 €
Description: Hardcover, color pictorial boards, in color pictorial dust jacket, 12" x 15". Note: German edition of *Soul Rebel*. A beautiful book filled with Burnett's photo sessions he had with Marley. Includes his firsthand accounts of meeting and photographing Bob Marley.

Title: *Soul Rebel: An Intimate Portrait of Bob Marley*
Author: David Burnett
Place of Publication: San Rafael, Calif., U.S.
Publisher: Insight Editions
Year: 2009: **ISBN-13:** 9781933784267
Pages: 142: **Price:** $39.95 U.S.
Description: Hardcover, color pictorial boards, lettered in white, in color pictorial dust jacket, 9.5" x 13". Note: A beautiful book filled with Burnett's photo sessions he had with Marley. Includes his firsthand accounts of meeting and photographing Bob Marley. Burnett was able to capture some interesting and unique photos of Marley.

Color pictorial cover board of Soul Rebel shown with no dust jacket.

Illustration

One great thing about Bob is that his message and music can be enjoyed by people of all ages and backgrounds. As a result, many illustrated books have been published around the world. Some of these books are geared towards children while other are aimed at the comic book loving audience. Most if not all of these books contain incredible illustrations by some very talented artists. Some of them, such as the Marvel Comic Books, were printed in standard comic book style while other used a more mainstream hardcover style. Several of these books, especially the ones geared for children, focus on Bob's early life. Illustration is another category that I believe can look forward to new releases for years to come.

Color Promo Card for I and I Bob Marley, Lee & Low Books 2009
www.jessewatson.com 4.25" x 6"

Title: *Reggae Rebel: La Vie de Bob Marley*
Author: Roland Monpierre
Place of Publication: Paris, France
Publisher: Editions Caribeennes
Year: 1988: **ISBN-10:** 2876790297
Pages: 65: **Price:** None Listed
Description: Hardcover, color pictorial boards, 8.75" x 11.25". Note: Marley's life from beginning to end in black and white illustrations.

Title: *Bob Marley: Tale of the Tuff Gong- Iron*
Author(s): Charles E. Hall, Illustrations by Gene Colan and Tennyson Smith
Place of Publication: New York, U.S.
Publisher: Marvel Music
Year: 1995: **ISBN-10:** 0785100776
Pages: 48: **Price:** $5.95 U.S.; $8.35 Canada
Description: Paperback with color pictorial wrappers, 6.5" x 10". Note: Tells Marley's story from birth through the late 1960s in a standard comic book style. Part one of a planned three part series.

Title: *Bob Marley: Tale of the Tuff Gong- Lion*
Author(s): Charles E. Hall, Illustrations by Gene Colan and Tennyson Smith
Place of Publication: New York, U.S.
Publisher: Marvel Music
Year: 1995: **ISBN-10:** 0785100768
Pages: 48: **Price:** $5.95 U.S.; $8.50 Canada
Description: Paperback with color pictorial wrappers, 6.5" x 10". Note: This edition picks up where *Iron* left off and continues the story through the Smile Jamaica Concert which was held on December 5th, 1976 at the National Heroes Park in Kingston, Jamaica. It was days before this concert that Marley was almost assassinated at his home on Hope Rd in Jamaica. Part two of three.

The third edition of Marvel Music's *Tale of Tuff Gong* titled *Zion* shown here was never published. A new book comprised of all three volumes in one has been shopped around to publishers for the past several years but has yet to generate interest.

Title: *La Legend De Bob Marley*
Author: Roland Monpierre
Place of Publication: France
Publisher: Source Publisher
Year: 2000: **ISBN-10:** 2884612696
Pages: 48: **Price:** 11 €
Description: Hardcover, color pictorial boards, 8.5" x 11.5". Note: Marley's life presented in cartoon style illustrations.

Title: *Bob Marley*
Author: Roland Monpierre
Place of Publication: Gentilly, France
Publisher: Eise Music
Year: 2001: **ISBN:** en cours / None Listed
Pages: 48: **Price:** None Listed
Description: Hardcover, color pictorial boards, 8.5" x 11.5". Note: Tells the story of Bob, Peter and Bunny in color illustrated form. Also includes information about reggae, Jamaica and other important roots figures.

Title: *The Boy From Nine Miles: The Early Life of Bob Marley*
Author(s): Cedella Marley and Gerald Hausman, Art by Mariah Fox
Place of Publication: Charlottesville, Va., U.S.
Publisher: Hampton Roads Publishing Co. Inc.
Year: 2002: **ISBN-10:** 1571742824
Pages: 55: **Price:** $17.95 U.S.
Description: Hardcover, color pictorial boards in color pictorial dust jacket, 7.5" x 9.25". Note: This is the story of Bob Marley's early life. Geared towards elementary aged children, it is a great introduction to Bob. Nesta Robert Marley was born on February 6, 1945 in Rhoden Hall, JA. He was born to an 18-year-old black Jamaican girl and a 63-year-old white Jamaican man.

Title: *Bob Marley: La star legendaire du reggae*
Author(s): Prof Lu and Marianne Maury-Kauffmann-Illustrations
Place of Publication: France
Publisher: Cauris
Year: 2004: **ISBN-10:** 2914605153
Pages: 24: **Price:** 5 €
Description: Paperback with color pictorial wrappers, 6.25" x 7". Note: A quick illustrated journey through the life of Marley.

Title: *Bob Marley: La Legend Des Wailers*
Author: Roland Monpierre
Place of Publication: Paris, France
Publisher: SeFam
Year: 2006: **ISBN-10:** 2226171274
Pages: 50: **Price:** 12,50 €
Description: Hardcover, color pictorial boards, 9.5" x 12.5". Note: This book tells the story of The Wailers from the beginning through their signing with Island Records in 1972. Illustrated with color drawings.

Title: *Bob Marley: Die Legende Der Wailers*
Author: Roland Monpierre (Translation: Uwe Lohmann)
Place of Publication: Koln, Germany
Publisher: Ehapa Comic Collection
Year: 2006: **ISBN-10:** 3770429192
Pages: 48: **Price:** 8,50 €
Description: Paperback with color pictorial wrappers, 6.5" x 10.25". Note: German edition of *La Legende Des Wailers*. Tells the story of The Wailers through their signing with Island Records in 1972. Illustrated with color drawings.

Title: *Three Little Birds (Adapted from the songs of Bob Marley)*
Author(s): Cedella Marley and Gerald Hausman (Mariah Fox-illustrations / artwork)
Place of Publication: Miami, U.S.
Publisher: Tuff Gong Books
Year: 2006: **ISBN-10:** 0971975825
Pages: 14: **Price:** None Listed
Description: Hardcover, color pictorial boards, 5.5" x 7". Note: Aimed at very young readers or listeners, this short story teaches the kids to not worry because every little thing is going to be alright. Filled with beautiful artwork.

Title: *Bob Marley: The Life of a Musical Legend*
Author(s): Gary Jeffrey & illustrated by Terry Riley
Place of Publication: New York, U.S.
Publisher: Rosen Central Publishing Group, Inc.
Year: 2007: **ISBN-10:** 1404208542
Pages: 48: **Price:** None Listed
Description: Hardcover, color pictorial boards, 7" x 10.25". Note: An illustrated look at the life and accomplishments of Bob Marley. Part of the 'Graphic Biographies' series.

Title: *Bob Marley: The Life of a Musical Legend*
Author(s): Gary Jeffrey & illustrated by Terry Riley
Place of Publication: New York, U.S.
Publisher: Rosen Publishing Group Ltd.
Year: 2007: **ISBN-10:** 1404209174
Pages: 48: **Price:** None Listed
Description: Paperback with color pictorial wrappers, 6.75" x 10". Note: An illustrated look at the life and accomplishments of Bob Marley. Part of the 'Graphic Biographies' series.

Title: *Bob Marley: The Life of a Musical Legend*
Author(s): Gary Jeffery & illustrated by Terry Riley
Place of Publication: London, UK and Sydney, Australia
Publisher: Franklin Watts
Year: 2007: **ISBN-10:** 0749677813
Pages: 48: **Price:** [?]
Description: Hardcover, color pictorial boards, 7" x 10.5". Note: An illustrated look at the life and accomplishments of Bob Marley. Part of the 'Graphic Biographies' series.

Title: *Bob Marley: La Legend Du Lion*
Author: Roland Monpierre
Place of Publication: Grenoble, France
Publisher: Vent Des Savanes
Year: 2008: **ISBN-13:** 9782356260024
Pages: 50: **Price:** 12,50 €
Description: Hardcover, color pictorial boards, 9.5" x 12.5". Note: Tells Marley's story from 1972 to his funeral services in 1981. Illustrated with color drawings. Marley passed away from melanoma cancer on May 11, 1981 in a Miami hospital. He was given a full state funeral for which the entire island of Jamaica turned out for. He is laid to rest in his mausoleum in Nine Miles, JA. It is next to the small house in which Marley grew up in.

Title: *I And I Bob Marley*
Author(s): Tony Medina and Jesse Joshua Watson-illustrations
Place of Publication: New York, U.S.
Publisher: Lee & Low Books Inc.
Year: 2009: **ISBN-13:** 9781600602573
Pages: 22: **Price:** $19.95 U.S.
Description: Hardcover, color pictorial boards in color pictorial dust jacket, 9.25" x 11.25". Note: The story of Marley's life told in a poetic style accompanied by some great paintings of Marley and The Wailers by Watson.

Title: *Bob Marley: The Life of a Musical Legend*
Author(s): Gary Jeffrey & illustrated by Terry Riley
Place of Publication: London, UK and Sydney, Australia
Publisher: Franklin Watts
Year: 2009: **ISBN-13:** 9780749689315
Pages: 48: **Price:** £6.99 UK
Description: Paperback with color pictorial wrappers, 6.75" x 10". Note: An illustrated look at the life and accomplishments of Bob Marley. Part of the 'Graphic Biographies' series.

Title: *Bob Marley: en bandes dessinees*
Author(s): Stephane Nappez (Various illustrators)
Place of Publication: Darnetal, France
Publisher: Petit a Petit
Year: 2009: **ISBN-13:** 9782849491607
Pages: 256: **Price:** 25 €
Description: Paperback with color pictorial wrappers, 6.5" x 9.25". Note: Title translation: Songs in Cartoons. The life of Bob is told in cartoon form. Several artists illustrate each phase of Marley's life while Nappez provides the text.

Non-English Biographies

If one wants to see the impact Bob Marley has made on the world they need not look any farther than the vast amount of books that have been published about him internationally. From Japan to Sweden, Brazil to Italy, books about Bob have been published in all four corners of the world. From 1977 to 1980 Bob Marley and The Wailers toured the world. Essentially what Bob did was go around the globe planting his reggae seeds. Those seeds have now grown into full mature trees and the books in this chapter could be considered the fruits of those trees. While some are translated versions of English biographies many others are original books written by native authors. Bob toured Europe heavily over the years and countries such as Italy, France, Spain and Germany have churned out a tremendous number of books. Because I am a U.S. based collector this was by far the hardest section of books on which to get complete and accurate information. Many of the included books had limited copies produced and are therefore extremely hard to obtain.

This section would not have been possible without the help of my reggae comrades from around the world. I want to thank all of my friends and fellow Marley lovers at Bob Marley Magazine.com for helping me with details and adding to the book section that Marco Virgona and I started. Much love and thanks to Marco and Ivan Serra for all of their hard work and dedication. I want to thank Fred Perry in France for setting up the first version of my Marley bibliography at his website, www.reggaelover.free.fr, over five years ago. I also want to send a special thanks to Werner Kajnath for all of his assistance and for his fine Wailers website www.wailers.de.

The books in this chapter are arranged chronologically by publishing date and listed in alphabetical order by country of origin.

Color Advert for Spanish No Woman No Cry, Ediciones B 2004
Spanish Trade Magazine, 6" x 8.75"

Title: *Bob Marley: el profeta del reggae*
Author: Sawnie Burgos
Place of Publication: Buenos Aires, Argentina
Publisher: Distal
Year: 1998: **ISBN-10:** 9875020206
Pages: 64: **Price:** None Listed
Description: Paperback with color pictorial wrappers, 7.75" x 11". Note: A biography illustrated with black and white photos. Includes a bibliography, video list, discography and timeline.

Title: *Rastafaris: La Mistica De Bob Marley*
Author: Dario Bermudez
Place of Publication: Buenos Aires, Argentina
Publisher: Editorial Kier
Year: 2005: **ISBN-10:** 9501770354
Pages: 159: **Price:** None Listed
Description: Paperback with color pictorial wrappers, 5.5" x 7.75". Note: A lesson in reggae, Rastafari and Marley. Illustrated with color photos from the author's personal collection.

Title: *Bob Marley: begirunea, maitasuna eta askatasuna*
Author: Artiz Usandizago
Place of Publication: Navarra, Basque
Publisher: Txalaparta Tafalla
Year: 2002: **ISBN-10:** 8481362662
Pages: 76: **Price:** 10 €
Description: Paperback with color pictorial wrappers. Note: Talks about reggae, Jamaica and Marley. Illustrated with black and white drawings.

Title: Sur Le Chemin De Retour: (Poems) *En Memoire de Robert Bob Marley, Fils de la Jamaique*
Author: G. Mahougnon David Daniel
Place of Publication: Porto-Novo, Benin
Publisher: Les Arts Avocetta
Year: 1981: **ISBN:** None
Pages: 51: **Price:** None Listed
Description: Paperback with pictorial wrappers, 5.5"x 8". Note: A collection of poems about Marley's life.

Title: *Bob Marley*
Author(s): Cassiano S. Quilici and Mateus Sampaio
Place of Publication: Sao Paulo, Brazil
Publisher: Editora Brasiliense
Year: 1982: **ISBN:** [?]
Pages: 82: **Price:** [?]
Description: First edition, paperback with color pictorial wrappers 4.75" x 6.25". Note: Includes a short biography and album list.

Title: *Bob Marley*
Author(s): Cassiano S. Quilici and Mateus Sampaio
Place of Publication: Sao Paulo, Brazil
Publisher: Editora Brasiliense
Year: 1983: **ISBN:** [?]
Pages: 82: **Price:** [?]
Description: Second edition, paperback with color pictorial wrappers, 4.75" x 6.25". Note: Includes a short biography and album list.

Title: *Queimando Tudo: A biografia definitive de Bob Marley*
Author(s): Timothy White (Translation: Ricardo Silveira and Antonio Selvaggi)
Place of Publication: Sao Paulo, Brazil
Publisher: Editor Record
Year: 1999: **ISBN:** 8501048216
Pages: 546: **Price:** R$ 69,90
Description: First printing, paperback with color pictorial wrappers, 6" x 9". Note: Brazilian edition of *Catch a Fire*. Title translation: Burning Everything- The Definitive Biography of Bob Marley. Was reprinted in 2006.

Title: Bob Marley: por ele mesmo
Author: Marco Antonio Cordosa
Place of Publication: Sao Paulo, Brazil
Publisher: Martin Claret
Year: 2004: **ISBN-10:** 857232108x
Pages: 176: **Price:** None Listed
Description: Paperback with color pictorial wrappers, 7.25" x 4.75". Note: Biography about Marley, Includes transcripts of interviews from the likes of Stephen Davis and Greg Brousser. Illustrated with black and white photos of Marley. Title trans: Bob Marley: By Himself.

Title: *No Woman No Cry (Minha vida con Bob Marley)*
Author(s): Rita Marley with Hettie Jones
Place of Publication: Sao Paulo, Brazil
Publisher: Planeta do Brazil
Year: 2004: **ISBN:** 8589885453
Pages: 240: **Price:** R$ 45,00
Description: Paperback with color pictorial wrappers, 6" x 9". Note: Brazilian edition of *No Woman No Cry*. Marley's wife describes her relationship with Bob from beginning to end and her own life as a musician and business woman.

Title: *Bob Marley: Talkin' Blues*
Author: Sergio Santana Archbold
Place of Publication: Medellin, Colombia
Publisher: Ediciones Salsa y Cultura
Year: 1996: **ISBN:** None
Pages: 198: **Price:** None Listed
Description: Paperback with color pictorial wrappers, 6.5" x 9". Note: Overview of Marley life and music. Talks about the Smile Jamaica Concert, One Love Peace Concert, Zimbabwe shows and Marley's last days in Germany. Contains extracts from various interviews and is illustrated with black and white photos. Includes a glossary, discography, players of instruments list, video list, bibliography and lyrics to 18 songs in English and Spanish. 1000 copies printed

Title: *Peter Tosh: El Ministro Del Reggae*
Author: Sergio Santana Archbold
Place of Publication: Medellin, Colombia
Publisher: Ediciones Salsa y Cultura
Year: 1994: **ISBN:** None
Pages: 130: **Price:** None Listed
Description: Paperback with color pictorial wrappers, 5.25" x 7.75". Note: A chronological look at Tosh's life and music. Talks about his incredible performance and speech at the One Love Peace Concert as well as his assassination in 1987. Includes a basic discography and lyric transcriptions to 24 songs. Illustrated with black and white photos. 1000 copies printed

Title: Ohen v Dlanich: Zivot Bobo Marleyho
Author(s): Timothy White (Translation: Sonya Tobiasova)
Place of Publication: Olomouc, Czech Republic
Publisher: Votobia
Year: 1998: **ISBN-10:** 8072200143
Pages: 476 **Price:** [?]
Description: Paperback with color pictorial wrappers, 5.5" x 7.75". Note: Czech edition of Catch a Fire. Title translation is *Fire in His Hands. Life of Bob Marley.*

Title: *Bob Marley: Mies, Musiikki & Mystiikka*
Author: Kari Kosmos
Place of Publication: Helsinki, Finland
Publisher: Like Kustannus Oy Ltd.
Year: 1999: **ISBN-10:** 9515786452
Pages: 205: **Price:** 23 €
Description: First edition, paperback with color pictorial wrappers. Note: Marley biography in Finish. Illustrated with black and white photographs. Title trans: Man, Music & Mysticism.

Title: *Bob Marley: Mies, Musiikki & Mystiikka*
Author: Kari Kosmos
Place of Publication: Helsinki, Finland
Publisher: WOSY
Year: 2007: **ISBN-13:** 9789510328873
Pages: 232: **Price:** 32 €
Description: Second edition, paperback with color pictorial wrappers. Note: A Marley biography that traces his life from beginning to end. Also explains Rastafari to the Finish reader. Illustrated with photos. Part of the Johnny Kniga series. Title trans: Man, Music & Mysticism.

Title: *Bob Marley: le rasta*
Author: Marc Payen
Place of Publication: Paris, France
Publisher: Encre
Year: 1981: **ISBN-10:** 2864181142
Pages: 122: **Price:** 65 F
Description: Paperback with color pictorial wrappers, 8" x 11". Note: Early French biography about Marley.

Title: *Bob Marley*
Author(s): Stephen Davis (Translation: Helene Lee)
Place of Publication: Paris, France
Publisher: Lieu Commun
Year: 1991: **ISBN-10:** 2867051495
Pages: 400: **Price:** 128 F
Description: First French edition, paperback with color pictorial wrappers, 6" x 9". Note: French edition of Davis' classic Bob Marley biography. Title page states that this is the sixth edition. Also states a 1991 copyright from an expanded edition. This book has been extremely successful in France.

Title: *Bob Marley*
Author(s): Stephen Davis (Translation: Helene Lee)
Place of Publication: Paris, France
Publisher: Seuil
Year: 1992: **ISBN-10:** 2020146576
Pages: 401: **Price:** None Listed
Description: Second printing, paperback with color pictorial wrappers, 4.25" x 7". Note: Second French printing of Davis' Classic biography. Includes a discography by Olivier Albot.

Title: *Bob Marley*
Author: Margaret E. Ward
Place of Publication: Paris, France
Publisher: Hors Collection
Year: 1994: **ISBN-10:** 2258038812
Pages: 79: **Price:** 79 F
Description: Hardcover, color pictorial boards, 9.25" x 12.25". Note: French version of Ward's 1993 book. A short juvenile biography about Marley with color and black and white photos.

Title: *Bob Marley: legende rasta*
Author(s): Chris Salewicz and Adrian Boot
Place of Publication: Paris, France
Publisher: Seuil
Year: 1995: **ISBN-10:** 2020218291
Pages: 288: **Price:** [?]
Description: First French edition, hardcover, full black cloth, gilt, in color pictorial dust jacket, 10" x 10.25". Note: French edition of Songs of Freedom. This book contains lots of vivid photographs as well as informative text. Released in conjunction with Island's four album box set of the same name. The official authorized biography.

Title: *Bob Marley: musicien, poete, militant, rasta prophete*
Author: Francis Dordor
Place of Publication: Paris, France
Publisher: Casterman
Year: 1997: **ISBN-10:** 2203238038
Pages: 45: **Price:** [?]
Description: Paperback with color pictorial wrappers, 4.5" x 5.5". Note: Short biography about Marley.

Title: *Bob Marley: L'histoire de Bob Marley la discographie commentee les photos. Le lexique des anecdotes*
Author: Erik Frank
Place of Publication: France
Publisher: L'express
Year: 1998: **ISBN-10:** 2843430097
Pages: 127: **Price:** 22 FF
Description: Paperback with color pictorial wrappers, 4" x 7". Note: French biography with a discography and photos.

Title: *Bob Marley*
Author: Francis Dordor
Place of Publication: Paris: France
Publisher: Librio Musique
Year: 1999: **ISBN-10:** 2277302783
Pages: 86: **Price:** 10 FF
Description: Paperback with color pictorial wrappers, 5.25" x 8". Note: French biography about Marley. Includes a discography, list of videos, films and internet sites. Was reprinted in 2002 with ISBN-10: 229031708x.

Title: *Bob Marley de A-Z*
Author: Herve Guilleminot
Place of Publication: Paris, France
Publisher: Les Guides Music Book
Year: 2003: **ISBN-10:** 2843430718
Pages: 122: **Price:** 5 €
Description: First edition, paperback with color pictorial wrappers, 4.25" x 6.75". Note: The story of Marley told in a dictionary / glossary style. Includes a discography and time line. Illustrated with black and white pictures of select album covers.

Title: *Bob Marley*
Author(s): Stephen Davis (Translation: Helene Lee)
Place of Publication: Paris, France
Publisher: Seuil- Points
Year: 2004: **ISBN-10:** 2020640201
Pages: 416: **Price:** 8 €
Description: Third printing, paperback with color pictorial wrappers, 4" x 7". Note: Third French printing of Davis' classic Bob Marley biography. Includes a discography by Olivier Albot.

Title: Bob Marley
Author(s): Stephen Davis (Translation: Helene Lee)
Place of Publication: Paris, France
Publisher: Editions du Seuil
Year: 2007: **ISBN-13:** 9782020640206
Pages: 402: **Price:** 8 €
Description: Fourth printing, paperback with color pictorial wrappers, 4.25" x 7". Note: Fourth French printing of Davis' classic Bob Marley biography. Includes a discography by Olivier Albot. Although I own this book it is hard to tell if it is a 2004 edition or a 2007 reprint of the 2004 edition. I believe it is a 2007 reprint as that is a way to explain the different covers.

Title: *Bob Marley: Le Reggae & Les Rastas Une histoire de la musique jamaicaine*
Author: Bruno Blum
Place of Publication: Paris, France
Publisher: Hors Collection Editions
Year: 2004: **ISBN-10:** 2258064775
Pages: 160: **Price:** 22 €
Description: Paperback with color pictorial wrappers, 7.5" x 10.25". Note: A history lesson in Marley, Jamaica, Rastafari and reggae- Jamaican and international. Illustrated with dozens of color photos, album covers and the authors own artwork. A jam packed book.

Title: *Ma vie avec Bob Marley...No Woman, No Cry*
Author(s): Rita Marley with Hettie Jones
Place of Publication: Paris, France
Publisher: City Editions
Year: 2004: **ISBN-10:** 2915320101
Pages: 236: **Price:** [?]
Description: Paperback with color pictorial wrappers, 6" x 9". Note: French edition of *No Woman No Cry*. Marley's wife describes her relationship with him from beginning to end and her own life as a musician and business woman.

Title: *Bob Marley*
Author: Francis Dordor
Place of Publication: Paris, France
Publisher: Librio Musique
Year: 2006: **ISBN-10:** 229033958x
Pages: 78: **Price:** 2 €
Description: Third edition, paperback with color pictorial wrappers, 5" x 8". Note: French biography about Marley. Includes lists of albums, videos, films and internet sites.

Title: *Bob Marley de A-Z*
Author: Herve Guilleminot
Place of Publication: Paris, France
Publisher: Group Express Editions
Year: 2005: **ISBN-10:** 2843432987
Pages: 116: **Price:** 6 €
Description: Second edition, paperback with color pictorial wrappers, 5" x 6.75". Note: The story of Marley told in a dictionary / glossary style. Includes a discography, time line and is illustrated with black and white pictures of select album covers. This edition includes updates.

Title: *Bob Marley: la Legende*
Author(s): James Henke (Translation: Philippe Paringaux)
Place of Publication: France
Publisher: editions du Panama
Year: 2006: **ISBN-10:** 2755700920
Pages: 64: **Price:** 45 €
Description: Hardcover, color pictorial boards, 9" x 10.75". Note: French edition of *Marley Legend*. Fully illustrated biography with removable memorabilia reproductions including Marley's notebook, handwritten lyrics and concert memorabilia. Comes with an interview CD.

Title: *Bob Marley: Collector*
Author: Delphine Sloan
Place of Publication: Saint-Victor-d'Epine, France
Publisher: City Editions
Year: 2006: **ISBN-10:** 291532090x
Pages: 112: **Price:** 13,50 €
Description: Hardcover with color pictorial boards, 6.75" x 9.75". Note: A French biography about Marley illustrated with color photos and album guide.

Title: *Sur La Route Avec Bob Marley: 1978-1980 Un Chevalier Blanc A Babylone*
Author(s): Bruno Blum and Mark Miller
Place of Publication: Paris, France
Publisher: Scali
Year: 2007: **ISBN-10:** 2350121666
Pages: 219: **Price:** 26 €
Description: Hardcover, 6" x 9.25". Note: Miller, Marley's stage manager from 1978-1980, tells stories of life on the road with Bob and The Wailers. Includes many unpublished photos. Title translation: On The Road with Bob Marley.

Title: *Bob Marley & The Wailers Exodus: Les 30 Ans*
Author: Richard Williams
Place of Publication: France
Publisher: EPA Editions
Year: 2007: **ISBN-10:** 2851206737
Pages: 142: **Price:** 29,90 €
Description: Hardcover, full red boards, gilt, in color pictorial dust jacket, 9.75" x 9.75". Note: French edition of *Exodus*. Released in conjunction with the 30th anniversary of the Exodus album, several contributing writers tell the story of *Exodus*. It is illustrated with several color and black and white photos and comes with the original album on CD.

Title: *Bob Marley: Le Prophete spiritual*
Author: Ian McCann
Place of Publication: France
Publisher: Music and Entertainment Books
Year: 2008: **ISBN-10:** 2357260025
Pages: 132: **Price:** 14,50 €
Description: Paperback with color pictorial wrappers, 6.25" x 9.25". Note: A new French edition of McCann's guide book. A guide to the music of Marley.

Title: *Bob Marley*
Author: Francis Dordor
Place of Publication: Paris, France
Publisher: Flammarion
Year: 2009: **ISBN-10:** 229033958x
Pages: 400: **Price:** 20,81 €
Description: Fourth edition, paperback with color pictorial wrappers, 6" x 9.25". Note: Updated French biography about Marley. Includes lists of albums, videos, films and internet sites.

Title: *Bob Marley: Rasta Reggae Rebellion*
Author: Henderson Dalrymple
Place of Publication: Munich, Germany
Publisher: Trinkot Verlag
Year: 1977: **ISBN-10:** 3881670068
Pages: 128: **Price:** None Listed
Description: Paperback with color pictorial wrappers, 5.25" x 8". Note: German edition of Dalrymple's early Marley biography. Illustrated with black and white photos and a German Island Records advert for *Exodus*. This is probably the first German Bob Marley book.

Title: *Bob Marley*
Author: Manfred Evert
Place of Publication: Germany
Publisher: Pro Verlag
Year: 1981: **ISBN-10:** 3887150015
Pages: 176: **Price:** 6,80 DM Germany; 7 SFR Switzerland
Description: Paperback with color pictorial wrappers, 5.75" x 8.25". Note: Early German biography about Marley.

Title: *Bob Marley: Reggae, Rastafari Ein Kurzes, Schnelles Leben*
Author(s): Timothy White (Translation: Teja Schwaner)
Place of Publication: Munich, Germany
Publisher: Heyne Verlag
Year: 1983, 1984, 1989: **ISBN-10:** 3453350367
Pages: 397: **Price:** [?]
Description: Paperback with color pictorial wrappers, 7" x 10". Note: First German edition of Catch a Fire. Illustrated with black and white photos. 1983 edition shown. Title trans: A Short, Fast Life.

Title: *Bob Marley: Rebell und Botschafter des Reggae (Catch a Fire)*
Author: Timothy White
Place of Publication: Hofen, Germany
Publisher: Hannibal Verlag
Year: 1993: **ISBN-10:** 385445077x
Pages: 422: **Price:** None Listed
Description: Fourth German edition, hardcover with color pictorial boards. Note: German edition of *Catch a Fire*. Illustrated with black and white photos. Title translation: Rebel and ambassador of Reggae.

Title: *Bob Marley: Mythos, Musik & Rastas*
Author: Henderson Dalrymple
Place of Publication: Markt Erlbach, Germany
Publisher: Raymond Martin Verlag
Year: 1993: **ISBN-10:** 3886312127
Pages: 112: **Price:** [?]
Description: Second German edition, paperback with color pictorial wrappers. Note: A later German edition of Dalrymple's early biography.

Title: *Do the Reggae: Reggae von Pocomania bis ragamuffin und der Mythos Bob Marley*
Author: Rene Wynands
Place of Publication: Germany
Publisher: Piper, Mainz, Shoft
Year: 1995: **ISBN-10:** 349218409x
Pages: 243: **Price:** [?]
Description: Paperback with color pictorial wrappers. Note: Information on Jamaican music with emphasis on the music of Bob Marley.

Title: *Bob Marley: Konig des Reggae*
Author: Robert Kopp
Place of Publication: Markt Erlbach, Germany
Publisher: Raymond Martin Verlag
Year: 1996: **ISBN-10:** 3886312275
Pages: 176: **Price:** None Listed
Description: Paperback with color pictorial wrappers, 5.75" x 8.25". Note: Lyrics to 39 Marley songs with German translations. Title trans: King of Reggae.

Title: *Bob Marley: in eighenten worten*
Author(s): Ian McCann (Translation: Max Herre and Ursula Damn)
Place of Publication: Heidelberg, Germany
Publisher: Palmyra Verlag
Year: 2000: **ISBN-10:** 3930378299
Pages: 115: **Price:** None Listed
Description: Hardcover, color pictorial boards, 8.5" x 5.5". Note: German edition of *In His Own Words*. A collection of quotes from Marley on different topics. Illustrated with black and white photos.

Title: *Bob Marley: Catch A Fire*
Author(s): Timothy White (Translation: Teja Schwaner and Roland M. Hahn)
Place of Publication: Hofen, Germany
Publisher: Hannibal Verlag GmGH
Year: 2000: **ISBN 10:** 385445077x
Pages: 422: **Price:** [?]
Description: Fifth German edition, paperback with color pictorial wrappers. Note: German edition of Catch a Fire.

Title: *Trench Town sehen und sterben: die Bob Marley Jahre*
Author: Helene Lee
Place of Publication: Hofen, Germany
Publisher: Hannibal
Year: 2005: **ISBN-10:** 3854452543
Pages: 283: **Price:** [?]
Description: Paperback with color pictorial wrappers, 5.25" x 8.25". Note: A Look at Jamaica's capital city and the violence it has endured throughout the years. Explores Marley's upbringing there and the impact it had on his life.

Title: *No Woman No Cry: Mein Leben Mit Bob Marley*
Author(s): Rita Marley with Hettie Jones (Translation: Silvia Morawetz and Werner Schmitz)
Place of Publication: Hamburg, Germany
Publisher: Rockbuch Verlag / Buhmann und Haeseler
Year: 2005: **ISBN-10:** 9783927638075
Pages: 287: **Price:** 19,90 €
Description: Hardcover, black quarter cloth and grey boards, lettered in silver, in color pictorial dust jacket, 5.5" x 8.75". Note: German edition of *No Woman No Cry*. Marley's wife describes her relationship with him from beginning to end and her own life as a musician and business woman.

Title: *Marley Legend: Die Legende*
Author(s): James Henke (Translation: Annie Litvin)
Place of Publication: Berlin, Germany
Publisher: Schwarzkopf & Schwarzkopf
Year: 2006: **ISBN-13:** 9783896026811
Pages: 64: **Price:** 29,90 €
Description: Hardcover, color pictorial boards, 10" x 11". Note: German edition of *Marley Legend*. Fully illustrated biography with removable memorabilia reproductions including Marley's notebook, handwritten lyrics and concert memorabilia. Comes with an interview CD.

Title: *Exodus: Bob Marley & The Wailers Exil 1977 Sonderausgate Zum 30, Jahrestag*
Author(s): Richard Williams (Translation: Teja Schwaner, Henning Dedekind, Paul Schwanker)
Place of Publication: Hofen, Germany
Publisher: Hannibal
Year: 2007: **ISBN-10:** 385445287x
Pages: 142: **Price:** [?]
Description: Hardcover, full red boards, gilt, in color pictorial dust jacket, 9.75" x 9.75". Note: German edition of *Exodus*. Released in conjunction with the 30th anniversary of the *Exodus* album, several contributing writers tell the story of *Exodus*. It is illustrated with several color and black and white photos and comes with the original album on CD.

Title: Bob Marley: Rasta Reggae
Author: Henderson Dalrymple
Place of Publication: Athens, Greece
Publisher: Apopira Publications
Year: 1983: **ISBN-10:** 9607034325
Pages: 108: **Price:** None Listed
Description: Paperback with color pictorial wrappers, 5" x 8". Note: Greek edition of Dalrymple's early Marley biography illustrated with black and white photos. ISBN on the title page is listed as 9607034327. ISBN on the back cover is listed as 9607034325.

Title: *Bob Marley*
Author: Dimitra Andriopoulou
Place of Publication: Greece
Publisher: Route Panos-Cigarettes
Year: 1997: **ISBN-10:** 9607716043
Pages: 79: **Price:** None Listed
Description: Paperback with pictorial wrappers, 5.5" x 8". Note: Short biography, lyrics to 14 songs in English and Greek, illustrated with black and white photos. This book is in 100% Greek.

Title: *Bob Marley*
Author: George Staois
Place of Publication: Thessaloniki, Greece
Publisher: Katsanos Books
Year: 1991?: **ISBN:** None Listed
Pages: 223: **Price:** None Listed
Description: Paperback with color pictorial wrappers, 5.5" x 8". Note: A short biography followed by the lyrics to 73 songs in both English and Greek. Includes a 15 page discography in the back. Book is in 100% Greek with no ISBN or date. I translated what I could to get all above information.

Title: *H Zoh Moy Me Ton Bob Marley: No Woman, No Cry*
Author(s): Rita Marley with Hettie Jones
Place of Publication: St. Anargyroi, Greece
Publisher: Ankara
Year: 2004: **ISBN-13:** 9604223518
Pages: 236: **Price:** [?]
Description: Paperback with color pictorial wrappers, 6" x 9". Note: Greek edition of *No Woman No Cry*. Marley's wife describes her relationship with Bob him from beginning to end and her own life as a musician and business woman.

Title: *Bob Marley*
Author: Mohamed El-Fers
Place of Publication: Amsterdam, Netherlands
Publisher: Passa Tempo
Year: 1991: **ISBN-10:** 9053300155
Pages: 94: **Price:** None Listed
Description: Paperback with color pictorial wrappers, 4.5" x 6.75". Note: Short Dutch biography. Includes a time line and bibliography.

Title: *Dunia Dalam Ganja: dari ACEH hingga Bob Marley*
Author: Abdul Khalik
Place of Publication: Indonesia
Publisher: Pinus Book Publisher
Year: 2007: **ISBN-10:** 979990109x
Pages: 236: **Price:** [?]
Description: Paperback with color pictorial wrappers, 4.75" x 7.5". Note: More or less a book about the medicinal qualities of herb. Includes information about Rastafari and Bob Marley. Title trans.: World in Cannabis: from ACEH to Bob Marley.

Title: *Bob Marli: Sipur Hayav*
Author(s): Cedella Marley Booker with Anthony Winkler (Translation: Gil Bunshtain)
Place of Publication: Tel-Aviv, Israel
Publisher: Modan Publisher House
Year: 2001: **ISBN-10:** None Listed
Pages: 293: **Price:** None Listed
Description: Paperback with color pictorial wrappers, 5.5" x 8.25". Note: Israeli edition of *Bob Marley: An Intimate Portrait by His Mother.* The autobiography of Marley's mother, Cedella Marley-Booker, and her personal accounts of Bob's life. Includes details about Bob's agonizing final days in Germany. Illustrated with personal photos.

Title: *Bob Marley: canzoni*
Author: Ernesto Assante
Place of Publication: Rome, Italy
Publisher: Lato Side
Year: 1979: **ISBN:** None
Pages: 159: **Price:** L. 3,500
Description: Hardcover, color pictorial boards, 5.5" x 7.5". Note: Book of lyrics.

Title: *Peter Tosh: canzoni*
Author: Andrea D'Anna
Place of Publication: Rome, Italy
Publisher: Lato Side
Year: 1980: **ISBN:** None
Pages: 82: **Price:** [?]
Description: Hardcover, color pictorial boards, 4.75" x 7.5". Note: Book of Peter Tosh lyrics.

Title: Bob Marley: Canzoni di liberta
Author: Marco Grompi
Place of Publication: Florence, Italy
Publisher: Giunti Gruppo Editoriale
Year: 1997: **ISBN-10:** 8809212061
Pages: 127: **Price:** L. 8,000
Description: Paperback with color pictorial wrappers, 5.5" x 5". Note: A chronological list of releases with detailed notes about the Island releases through 1995.

Title: Bob Marley: Il mito del reggae
Author: Gianni Lucini
Place of Publication: Italy
Publisher: Sonzogno
Year: 1999: **ISBN-13:** 9788848600255
Pages: 64: **Price:** [?]
Description: Paperback with color pictorial wrappers. Note: Title translation: The Myth of Reggae. A color picture book with biography and unpublished anecdotes and curiosities. Comes with CD.

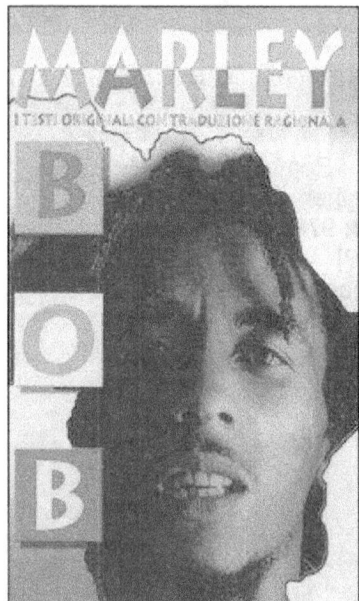

Title: *Bob Marley: I Testi Originali Con Traduzione Ragionata*
Author: N/A
Place of Publication: Italy
Publisher: Lo Vecchio
Year: 2000: **ISBN-10:** 8873330541
Pages: 270: **Price:** [?]
Description: Paperback with color pictorial wrappers. Note: Book of lyrics. Title Translation: The Original Texts with Translations

Title: La Storia dietro ogni Canzone di Bob Marley
Author: Anthony Arnold
Place of Publication: Italy
Publisher: Strade Blu
Year: 2001: **ISBN-10:** 8888116044
Pages: 337: **Price:** [?]
Description: 7.75" x 11". Note: Title translation: The Story behind each song by Bob Marley. A list of songs and the background information.

Title: *Bob Marley: Una Vita di Fuoco*
Author(s): Timothy White (Translation: Alessandro Achilli)
Place of Publication: Italy
Publisher: Feltrinelli
Year: 2002: **ISBN-10:** 8807816792
Pages: 356: **Price:** [?]
Description: Second edition, paperback with color pictorial wrappers. Note: Italian edition of Catch a Fire. Title Translation: A Life of Fire. The first 330 page edition was published in 1994 by Arcana Gruppo editorial in Milan, Italy with ISBN-10: 8879660284.

Title: *Le Canzoni Di Bob Marley*
Author: Marco Grompi
Place of Publication: Rome, Italy
Publisher: Editori Riuniti
Year: 2003: **ISBN-10:** 8835956056
Pages: 399: **Price:** [?]
Description: Paperback with color pictorial wrappers, 5.5" x 8.25". Note: An analysis of Marley's lyrics and biographical information. Title translation: The Songs of Bob Marley.

Title: *Le Lacrime di Bob Marley: No Woman No Cry Told to Massimo Cotto*
Author: Massimo Cotto
Place of Publication: Rome, Italy
Publisher: Elle U Multimedia
Year: 2004: **ISBN-10:** 8874762410
Pages: 80: **Price:** [?]
Description: Paperback with color pictorial wrappers. Note: Title Translation: The Tears of Bob Marley

Title: *No Woman No Cry: La Mia Vita Con Bob Marley*
Author(s): Rita Marley with Hettie Jones
Place of Publication: Italy
Publisher: Mondadori
Year: 2004: **ISBN-10:** 8804511400
Pages: 237: **Price:** [?]
Description: Paperback with color pictorial wrappers 6" x 9". Note: Italian edition of *No Woman No Cry*. Marley's wife describes her relationship with him from beginning to end and her own life as a musician and business woman.

Title: *Bob Marley and The Wailers: Exile 1977 Edizione del 30 Anniversario*
Author: Richard Williams
Place of Publication: Italy
Publisher: White Star
Year: 2007: **ISBN-10:** 8854008532
Pages: 144: **Price:** 29,90 €
Description: Hardcover, full red boards, gilt, in color pictorial dust jacket, 13" x 15". Note: Italian edition of *Exodus*. Released in conjunction with the 30th anniversary of the *Exodus* album, several contributing writers tell the story of *Exodus*. It is illustrated with color and black and white photos and comes with the original album on CD.

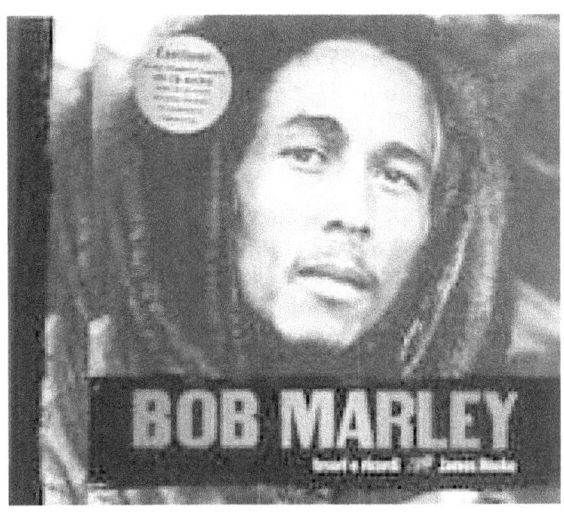

Title: *Bob Marley: tesori e ricordi*
Author: James Henke
Place of Publication: Italy
Publisher: White Star
Year: 2008: **ISBN-10:** 8854010197
Pages: 64: **Price:** 45 €
Description: Hardcover, color pictorial boards, 10" x 11". Note: Italian edition of *Marley Legend*. Fully illustrated biography with removable memorabilia reproductions including Marley's notebook, handwritten lyrics and concert memorabilia. Comes with an interview CD.

Title: *Bob Marley: In This Life*
Author(s): F.T. Sandman and Bob Marley
Place of Publication: Italy
Publisher: Chinaski Edizioni
Year: 2009: **ISBN-13:** 9788889966334
Pages: 180: **Price:** 12 €
Description: Paperback with color pictorial wrappers, 4.75" x 7.5". Note: A Collection of Marley interviews. Includes a look at Rastafari and the musical careers of Marley's children. Marley has several children who are talented and successful musicians: Ziggy, Sharon, Cedella, Stephen, Ky-Mani, Damian and Julian. Many of the other children work within the estate in some capacity.

Title: *Rasta Marley: Le Radici Del Reggae*
Author: Lorenzo Mazzoni
Place of Publication: Italy
Publisher: Nuovi Equilibri
Year: 2009: **ISBN-13:** 9788862220859
Pages: 218: **Price:** [?]
Description: Paperback with color pictorial wrappers. Note: Title translation: The Root of Reggae. This book is an analysis of 12 Marley songs and their relationship to Rastafari and the mystical vision that binds Rastas together.

Title: *Bob Marley: Tribute*
Author: Not Specified
Place of Publication: Rome, Italy
Publisher: Fratelli Spada
Year: 2009: **ISBN-10:** 8886992610
Pages: 96: **Price:** [?]
Description: Paperback with color pictorial wrappers. Note: A short biography with a discography and reviews of albums and tours. Part of the 'Rock Star' series

Title: *Song of Lion: Message Through Bob Marley*
Author: Bamboo Studio
Place of Publication: Japan
Publisher: Books Chaka
Year: 1989: **ISBN-10:** 4886960049
Pages: 144: **Price:** [?]
Description: Paperback with color pictorial wrappers, 7.25 x 10". Note: A Japanese look at the songs of Bob Marley.

Title: *Bob Marley And Jamaica*
Author(s): Malika Lee Whitney and Dermott Hussey (Translation: Yasumi Yamamoto; Foreword: Rita Marley)
Place of Publication: Japan
Publisher: Published Daiei
Year: 1995: **ISBN-10:** 4886825885
Pages: 231: **Price:** ¥ 3,200
Description: Paperback, full white paper binding, lettered in black, in color pictorial dust jacket, 9" x 12". Note: Title translation: Reggae Kingdom: Jamaica Bob Marley & The Holy Land. Japanese edition of *Bob Marley: Reggae King of the World.*

Title: *Bob Marley*
Author(s): Stephen Davis (Translation: Oohashi Yoshiko)
Place of Publication: Japan
Publisher: Shobunsha
Year: 1986: **ISBN-10:** 4794951884
Pages: 304: **Price:** ￥ 2,900
Description: Paperback with color pictorial wrappers, 6" x 8.75". Note: Title translation: Legendary Reggae. Japanese edition of Stephen Davis' *Bob Marley*.

Title: Vibes From Bob Marley
Author: Noa
Place of Publication: Japan
Publisher: Press Bureau JICC
Year: 1992: **ISBN-10:** 4796604200
Pages: 253: **Price:** [?]
Description: Paperback with color pictorial wrappers. Note: Translation of lyrics, tour map and biographical information.

Title: *Bob Marley: songs of freedom*
Author(s): Adrian Boot and Chris Salewicz (Translation: Nakae Masahiko; Executive editor: Rita Marley)
Place of Publication: Japan
Publisher: Blues Interaction, Inc.
Year: 1995: **ISBN-10:** 4938339153
Pages: 288: **Price:** ¥5,800
Description: Hardcover, full black cloth, gilt, in color pictorial wrappers, 10.5" x 10.5". Note: Japanese edition of *Songs of Freedom*. Published in a limited edition run of 4000 copies.

Title: *Bob Marley: in his own words*
Author(s): Ian McCann (Translation: Yamamoto Midori and Yasumi Yamamoto)
Place of Publication: Japan
Publisher: Uplink
Year: 1995: **ISBN-10:** 4309901395
Pages: 191: **Price:** [?]
Description: Paperback with color pictorial wrappers. Note: Title translation: Quotation Collection. Japanese edition of *Bob Marley: In His Own Words*. A collection of quotes from Marley on different topics.

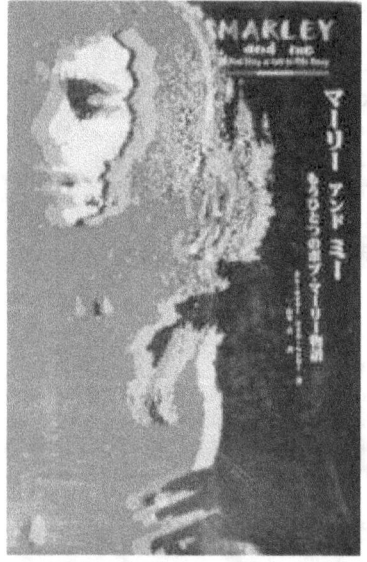

Title: *Marley and Me*
Author(s): Don Taylor with Mike Henry (Translation: Shiraki Mitsuqu)
Place of Publication: Japan
Publisher: M & S
Year: 1995: **ISBN-10:** 4896107020
Pages: 223: **Price:** [?]
Description: Paperback with color pictorial wrappers, 5.5" x 8.25". Note: Title translation: Bob Marley is Another Story. Japanese edition of *Marley and Me*. The autobiography of Don Taylor, one time manager of Bob Marley.

Title: *Bob Marley: Super Rock Guide*
Author(s): Ian McCann (Translation: Yamasaki Tomoyuki_
Place of Publication: Tokyo, Japan
Publisher: Shinko Music Entertainment [?]
Year: 1998: **ISBN:** 4401614895 [?]
Pages: 285: **Price:** [?]
Description: Note: Japanese edition of McCann's guide to Marley's music.

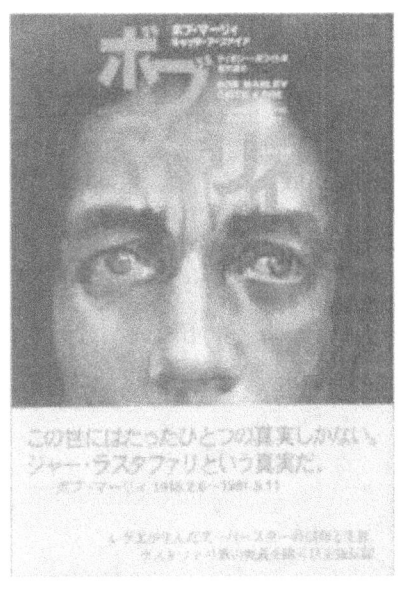

Title: *Bob Marley: Catch a Fire*
Author(s): Timothy White (Translation: Makoto Aoki)
Place of Publication: Japan
Publisher: Sha
Year: 1998: **ISBN-10:** 4276234956
Pages: 502: **Price:** [?]
Description: Paperback with color pictorial wrappers. Note: Japanese edition of *Catch a Fire: The Life of Bob Marley*. Title translation: Bobumaryi Catch a Fire.

Title: *Marley: The Illustrated Legend 1945-1981*
Author: Barry Lazell
Place of Publication: Tokyo, Japan
Publisher: Shinko Music Publishing Co. Ltd.
Year: 1996: **ISBN-10:** 4401615247
Pages: 80: **Price:** ¥ 1,500
Description: Paperback with color pictorial wrappers, 9" x 11.5". Note: Japanese edition of *Marley Legend*. A brief biography with several color photographs including some very rare ones.

Title: *Bob Marley: The World's Greatest Composers*
Author(s): Marsha Bronson (Translation: Gomi Yoshiko)
Place of Publication: Tokyo, Japan
Publisher: 偕成社
Year: 1999: **ISBN-10:** 4035423300
Pages: 183: **Price:** ¥ 1,905
Description: Paperback with color pictorial wrappers, 6" x 8.25". Note: Japanese edition of *Bob Marley: The World's Greatest Composers*. Title translation: Spread to the World the Legendary Reggae Musician.

Title: *Bob Marley File (Artist File 09)*
Author: Naoya Nakamura
Place of Publication: Tokyo,
Publisher: Shinko Music Publishing Co. Ltd.
Year: 2004: **ISBN-10:** 4401618785
Pages: 251: **Price:** ¥ 3,000
Description: Paperback, full black paper binding, lettered in grey, in color pictorial wrappers, 8.25" x 5.75". Note: Biography and album guide. Illustrated with several color photos of Bob Marley memorabilia and black and white album covers.

Title: *Bob Marley: One Love One Heart*
Author(s): Hirota Kanzi and Awazi Wako
Place of Publication: Japan
Publisher: Eight Companies
Year: 2004: **ISBN-10:** 4871642852
Pages: 207: **Price:** [?]
Description: Paperback with color pictorial wrappers, 8.25" x 11". Note: A Japanese biography of Marley.

Title: *Marley Legend: An Illustrated Life of Bob Marley*
Author(s): James Henke (Translation: Oshino Motoko)
Place of Publication: Japan
Publisher: Burusuintaakushonzu
Year: 2006: **ISBN-10:** 4860201477
Pages: 64: **Price:** [?]
Description: Hardcover, color pictorial boards, 10" x 10.75". Note: Japanese edition of *Marley Legend*. Fully illustrated biography with removable memorabilia reproductions including Marley's notebook, handwritten lyrics and concert memorabilia. Comes with an interview CD.

Title: *No Woman No Cry: My Life with Bob Marley*
Author(s): Rita Marley with Hettie Jones (Translation: Yamakawa Truth)
Place of Publication: Japan
Publisher: Kawade Shobo Shinsha
Year: 2005: **ISBN-10:** 4309268309
Pages: 262: **Price:** [?]
Description: Paperback with color pictorial wrappers, 5" x 7.5". Note: Japanese edition of *No Woman No Cry*. Marley's wife describes her relationship with him from beginning to end and her own life as a musician and business woman.

Title: *Bob Marley: The Complete Guide to His Music*
Author(s): Ian McCann, Harry Hawke and Ooishi Hazime (Translation: Okamoto Tiaki)
Place of Publication: Tokyo, Japan
Publisher: Shinko Music Publishing Co.
Year: 2006: **ISBN-10:** 4401630238
Pages: 313: **Price:** ¥1,785
Description: Paperback with color pictorial wrappers, 5" x 7.25". Note: Japanese edition of *Bob Marley: The Complete Guide to His Music*. An insightful and helpful guide to several of the officially released Marley albums.

Title: *Bob Marley*
Author(s): Stephen Davis (Translation: Yigyeongha)
Place of Publication: Korea
Publisher: Summer Hill
Year: 2007: **ISBN-13:** 9788990985316
Pages: 508: **Price:** ₩15,000 Korean
Description: Paperback with color pictorial wrappers, 5.75" x 8.5". Note: Korean edition of Davis' classic Bob Marley biography. Title translation is…well take your pick: *God was Born to Sing the Dead*; *Die as a God was Born to Sing*; *The Song was Born to Die as a God*; *Born to Sing the Dead*; *Songs to Die as a God was Born*; *Bob Marley was Born to Sing, God is Dead*; *Bob Marley was Born as a God is Dead* or *Bob Marley Song was Born to Die*.

Title: *Bob Marley*
Author: Marlene Gomez
Place of Publication: Cuauhtemoc, Mexico
Publisher: Editores Mexicanos Unidos, S.A.
Year: 2006: **ISBN-10:** 9681519167
Pages: 95: **Price:** None Listed
Description: Paperback with color pictorial wrappers, 5.5" x 8.25". Note: Biography about Marley with lyrics to several songs. Illustrated with black and white photos. Part of the 'Grande Personajes De La Musica Moderna' series.

Title: *Bob Marley: songs of freedom*
Author(s): Chris Salewicz en Adrian Boot (Translation: Joost van der Meer, Executive editor: Rita Marley)
Place of Publication: Netherlands
Publisher: Gravenhage
Year: 1995: **ISBN-10:** 9055010782
Pages: 288: **Price:** None Listed
Description: Hardcover, full black cloth, gilt, in color pictorial dust jacket, 9.5" x 12". Note: Dutch edition of *Songs of Freedom*. This book contains lots of vivid photographs and informative biographical text.

Title: *Bob Marley: Den Tredje Verdens Superstar*
Author: Sigbjørn Nedland
Place of Publication: Oslo, Norway
Publisher: Tiden Norsk
Date: 1988: **ISBN-10:** 8210030949
Pages: 125: **Price:** [?]
Description: Paperback with color pictorial wrappers. Note: Norwegian biography about Marley. Title translation: The Third World Superstar.

Title: Bob Marley: Catch A Fire- *Zycie Boba Marleya*
Author(s): Timothy White (Translation: Slawomir Golaszewski, Maciej Goralski, and Arthur Jarosinski)
Place of Publication: Warsaw, Poland
Publisher: Axis Mundi
Date: 2007: **ISBN-10:** 8392250788 (HC); 8392250761 (PB)
Pages: 550: **Price:** 49.00 zł
Description: Hardcover and paperback with color pictorial wrappers, 6" x 9". Note: Polish edition of *Catch a Fire*.

Title: *El Codigo Bob Marley: El Morya Sobre Bob Marley*
Author: Marilyn P.C.
Place of Publication: Puerto Rico
Publisher: Editorial Balance Arte / LuLu.com
Year: 2008: **ISBN-10:** 1435735137
Pages: 134: **Price:** [?]
Description: Paperback with color pictorial wrappers. Note: Short biography about Marley.

Title: *No Woman No Cry: Moia Zhizn's Bobom Marli*
Author(s): Rita Marley with Hettie Jones (Translation: Khetti Dzhous)
Place of Publication: Saint-Petersburg, Russia
Publisher: Amphora
Year: 2008: **ISBN-10:** 5367007716
Pages: 304: **Price:** [?]
Description: Paperback with color pictorial heavy stock wrappers, 5.25" x 8". Note: Russian edition of *No Woman No Cry*. Marley's wife describes her relationship with him from beginning to end and her own life as a musician and business woman. 5000 copies printed.

Title: *Bob Marley: Reggae-Ska-Pop-Rock*
Author: Jesus Ordova
Place of Publication: Barcelona, Spain
Publisher: Ediciones Jucar
Year: 1980: **ISBN-10:** 8433420410
Pages: 229: **Price:** [?]
Description: Paperback with color pictorial wrappers, 4.25" x 7". Note: Early Spanish biography about Marley.

Title: *Junto a los rios de babiliona biografia de Bob Marley*
Author: Josetxo Mintegi Irazusta
Place of Publication: Spain
Publisher: Editorial VOSA
Year: 1995: **ISBN-10:** 848218010x
Pages: 236: **Price:** [?]
Description: Paperback with color pictorial wrappers. Note: Spanish biography about Marley.

Title: *Bob Marley: Positive Vibration*
Author: Carlos Monty
Place of Publication: Valencia, Spain
Publisher: La Mascara
Year: 1995: **ISBN-10:** 8479745207
Pages: 80: **Price:** None Listed
Description: Paperback with color pictorial wrappers, 10.75" x 8". Note: A biography about Marley that is illustrated with several color and black and white photos.

Title: Bob Marley: Grandes Compositores del Mundo
Author: Marsha Bronson
Place of Publication: Madrid, Spain
Publisher: Edelvives
Year: 1996: **ISBN-10:** 8426335993
Pages: 64: **Price:** [?]
Description: Hardcover, color pictorial boards, 6.25" x 8.75". Note: Spanish edition of *Bob Marley: World's Greatest Composers.*

Title: *Bob Marley: Reggae*
Author: David F. Abel
Place of Publication: Valencia, Spain
Publisher: Todas la musicas
Year: 1997: **ISBN-10:** 8470742131
Pages: 238: **Price:** [?]
Description: Paperback with color pictorial wrappers. Note: A biography about Marley with guides to his songs and albums.

Title: *Bob Marley: Sa Vie Les Fans Anecdotes Chansons*
Author: Montana Vasquez
Place of Publication: Spain / France [?]
Publisher: Editions La Mascara / Tournon Editions
Year: 1999: **ISBN-10:** 8479746173
Pages: 119: **Price:** [?]
Description: Paperback with color pictorial wrappers, 5" x 5.5". Note: I do not own this book. I believe the text in French as the title is. The author and publisher are from Spain.

Title: *Bob Marley: Canciones 1*
Author: Various
Place of Publication: Madrid, Spain
Publisher: Editorial Fundamentos
Year: 1999: **ISBN-10:** 8424508463
Pages: 176: **Price:** [?]
Description: Paperback with color pictorial wrappers, 6" x 8". Note: Cover states 2nd edicion. Lyric transcriptions in English and Spanish.

Title: *Bob Marley: Canciones 2*
Author: Various
Place of Publication: Madrid, Spain
Publisher: Editorial Fundamentos
Year: 2000: **ISBN-10:** 8424508475
Pages: 176: **Price:** [?]
Description: Paperback with color pictorial wrappers, 6" x 8". Note: Lyric transcriptions in English and Spanish. Title page states: "second printing of first edition."

Title: *Bob Marley*
Author: Andres Lopez Martinez
Place of Publication: Madrid, Spain
Publisher: Catedra
Year: 2002: **ISBN-10:** 84377619947
Pages: 159: **Price:** None Listed
Description: Paperback with color pictorial wrappers, 4.25" x 7". Note: Biography, illustrated with black and white photos. Includes a discography, video list and time line.

Title: *No Woman No Cry: Mi vida junto a Bob Marley*
Author(s): Rita Marley with Hettie Jones (Translation: Merce Diago and Abel Debritto)
Place of Publication: Barcelona, Spain
Publisher: Ediciones B
Year: 2004: **ISBN-10:** 8466611312
Pages: 206: **Price:** 17,50 €
Description: Paperback, full white paper binding, lettered in black in color pictorial dust jacket, 6" x 9". Note: Spanish edition of *No Woman No Cry*. Marley's wife describes her relationship with him from beginning to end and her own life as a musician and business woman.

Title: *Trench Town Reggae: En Las Calles De Bob Marley*
Author: Helene Lee
Place of Publication: Barcelona, Spain
Publisher: Oceano
Year: 2005: **ISBN-10:** 8449426928
Pages: 263: **Price:** None
Description: Paperback with color pictorial wrappers, 6.25" x 9.25". Note: The story of Marley in conjunction with Jamaica and the political atmosphere.

Title: *Bob Marley: El Gran Icono De La Cultura Reggae, Un Musico Genialy un Simbolo De Liberacion*
Author(s): Timothy White (Translation: Joan Sardin and David Agusti Hernandez)
Place of Publication: Barcelona, Spain
Publisher: Robbin Book
Year: 2008: **ISBN-13:** 9788496222786
Pages: 560: **Price:** 29,50 €
Description: Paperback with color pictorial wrappers, 6.75" x 9.5". Note: Title translation: The Great Reggae Culture Icon, a Great Music and a Symbol of Liberation. Spanish edition of *Catch a Fire*.

Title: *Marley: Lejonets frihetssang*
Author: Christer Lindberg
Place of Publication: Lund, Sweden
Publisher: Arkiv forlag
Year: 2003: **ISBN-10:** 9179241603
Pages: 235: **Price:** None Listed
Description: Paperback with color pictorial wrappers, 6" x 7.25". Note: Title Translation: The Lions Freedom Song. A Swedish biography illustrated with black and white photos. Includes a select discography. This book has sold approximately 2000 copies in Sweden.

Title: *Falsata Mirindimo ya Bob Marley*
Author: Augustos S. Magege
Place of Publication: Dar es Salaam, Tanzania
Publisher: The Bismarocks
Year: 2006: **ISBN:** 9987909711
Pages: 170: **Price:** TZS 5,000
Description: Paperback with color pictorial wrappers, 8.25" x 11". Note: Title translation: The Philosophy of Bob Marley. In the Swahili language, this book tells the story of Marley's life and the history and philosophy of Rastafari. Magege translated into Swahili, lyrics to 12 Marley songs.

Title: *Bob Marley: Reggae*
Author: Burak Eldem
Place of Publication: Istanbul, Turkey
Publisher: IMGE
Year: 1985: **ISBN:** None
Pages: 219: **Price:** None Listed
Description: Paperback with color pictorial wrappers, 5" x 7.5". Note: Biography, lyrics to songs in English and Turkish, glossary and short discography.

Title: *Bob Marley: kendi sozleriyle*
Author: Ian McCann
Place of Publication: Istanbul, Turkey
Publisher: AFA Yayincilik
Year: 1995: **ISBN-10:** 9754142874
Pages: 96: **Price:** None printed on the book but does have a 350000 Turkish price tag on it.
Description: Paperback with color pictorial wrappers, 7" x 10". Note: Turkish edition of *Bob Marley: In His Own Words*. A collection of quotes from Marley on different topics.

Title: *No Woman No Cry: Bob Marley ile hayatim*
Author(s): Rita Marley with Hettie Jones (Translation: Ela Gurdemir)
Place of Publication: Istanbul, Turkey
Publisher: Citlembik Yayinlari
Year: 2005: **ISBN-10:** 9756663642
Pages: 216: **Price:** None
Description: Paperback with color pictorial wrappers, 5.75" x 8.5". Note: Turkish edition of *No Woman No Cry*. Bob's wife describes her relationship with him from beginning to end and her own life as a musician and business woman.

Title: *Efsanenin Dogusu Bob Marley*
Author: Christopher John Farley
Place of Publication: Instanbul, Turkey
Publisher: Bilge Kultur Sanat
Year: 2006: **ISBN-10:** 994442515x
Pages: 203: **Price:** None Listed
Description: Paperback with color pictorial wrappers, 5.25" x 8.5". Note: Turkish edition of *Before the Legend*. A fresh detailed look at the life of Bob Marley before fame and stardom. Follows Marley's life from birth through the release of *Catch a Fire* in 1973.

Additional Non English Books

Title: *Bob Marley: l'alibrary bindingum du souvenir*: **Author(s):** Adrian Boot and Vivien Goldman: **Place of Publication:** France: **Publisher:** Menges: **Year:** 1982: **ISBN-10:** 285620161x: **Pages:** 102: **Price:** [?]: **Description:** Paperback

Title: *Bob Marley: Legende Rasta (Songs of Freedom)*: **Author(s):** Adrian Boot and Chris Salewicz: **Place of Publication:** Paris, France: **Publisher:** Seuil: **Year:** 1998: **ISBN-10:** 2020218291: **Pages:** 288: **Price:** [?]: **Description:** Second French edition, Paperback, 10.25" x 10.5".

Title: *Bob Marley: Reggae King of the World (Die Interviews)*: **Author(s):** Malika Lee Whitney and Dermott Hussey (Translation: Hermann Moter; Foreword: Rita Marley): **Place of Publication:** Germany: **Publisher:** Minotaurus Projekt: **Year:** 1984: **ISBN-10:** 3921982200: **Pages:** 200: **Price:** [?]: **Description:** Paperback

Title: *Bob Marley*: **Author:** Chris Welch (Translation: Astrid Hartwig): **Place of Publication:** Germany: **Publisher:** Rastatt Moewig: **Year:** 1994: **ISBN-10:** 3811839802: **Pages:** 120: **Price:** [?]: **Description:** Paperback, 5" x 6".

Title: *Bob Marley: Songs of Freedom Die Bildbiographie*: **Author(s):** Adrian Boot and Chris Salewicz: **Place of Publication:** Germany: **Publisher:** Heyne: **Year:** 1995: **ISBN-10:** 3453087054: **Pages:** 288: **Price:** [?]: **Description:** Hardcover

Title: *Bob Marley*: **Author:** Margaret E. Ward: **Place of Publication:** Netherlands: **Publisher:** Ars Schibendi / Eke / ADC, Algemene Distributie Centrale: **Year:** 1994: **ISBN-10:** 905561016x: **Pages:** 64: **Price:** [?]: **Description:** 9.25" x 12.5"

Title: *Bob Marley: Canzoni di Liberta*: **Author:** Marco Grompi: **Place of Publication:** Italy: **Publisher:** Giunti Gruppi Editoriale: **Year:** 1997: **ISBN:** [?]: **Pages:** [?]: **Price:** [?]: **Description:** [?]

Songbooks

Given the incredible number of songs Bob wrote over the years it should come as no surprise that dozens of books have been published containing transcripts of his music. Songbooks were some of the earliest books published on Bob and to this day we continue to see more published every year.

The titles listed in this category are a very small sample of the many songbooks that have been published. Many seem to reprint the same most popular songs but a few here and there will venture out and publish the music to all of his gems. Some of the books in this section contain no music and are simply lyric books.

Black and white advert for The World of Reggae, Global Treasures 2001
The Beat Vol. 21 #5 2002, 3.5" x 5.75"

Title: *Bob Marley & The Wailers: Rastaman Vibration*
Author : Heather Harris (Photographs by Kim Gottlieb)
Place of Publication: U.S.
Publisher: Alamo Publications
Year: 1976: **ISBN:** None
Pages: 88: **Price:** $5.95 U.S.
Description: Paperback with color pictorial wrappers, 9" x 12". Note: Transcriptions to the *Rastaman Vibration* album as well as *I Shot the Sheriff*. One of the first Marley songbooks published.

Title: *Bob Marley & The Wailers*
Author: N/A
Place of Publication: London, UK
Publisher: Wise Publications
Year: 1976: **ISBN-10:** 0860012662
Pages: 94: **Price:** None Listed
Description: Paperback with color pictorial wrappers, 9" x 12". Note: Transcriptions to 17 Marley songs from the first four Island albums. One of the first Marley songbooks published.

Title: The Bob Marley & The Wailers Songbook
Author: N/A
Place of Publication: Hialeah, Fla., U.S.
Publisher: Columbia Pictures Publications and Alamo Publications
Year: 1981: **ISBN-10:** 089898078x
Pages: 104: **Price:** $12.95 U.S.
Description: Paperback with color pictorial wrappers, 9" x 12". Note: Transcriptions to 16 songs including *Forever Loving Jah*.

Title: *Robert Nesta Marley. 1945-1981 Ten Greatest Hits*
Author: N/A
Place of Publication: London, UK
Publisher: Wise Publications
Year: 1981: **ISBN-10:** 0860019667
Pages: 48: **Price:** None Listed
Description: Paperback with color pictorial wrappers, 9" x 12". Note: Transcriptions to ten classic songs.

Title: *Reggae Rocks the World: The Best of Reggae Music #1*: The Songs of *Peter Tosh*
Author: Arrangements by Leonard Moss
Place of Publication: Ojai, Calif., U.S.
Publisher: Creative Concepts Publishing Corp.
Year: 1992: **ISBN:** None
Pages: 32: **Price:** $11.95 U.S.
Description: Paperback with color pictorial wrappers, 9" x 12". Note: Transcriptions to Tosh's seminal album *Legalize It*. Tosh left The Wailers in 1974 and *Legalize It* was his first solo album. He continued to release music until his untimely murder in 1987. He is regarded worldwide as a musical legend and a founding father of reggae.

Title: *Bob Marley Best of Special Guitare Tablatures*
Author: N/A
Place of Publication: Paris, France
Publisher: Publication I.D. Music
Year: 1992: **ISBN:** None
Pages: 98: **Price:** None Listed
Description: Paperback with color pictorial wrappers, 9" x 12". Note: Transcriptions to 18 songs.

Title: *Legend: the best of Bob Marley and the Wailers*
Author: Colin Wells
Place of Publication: London, UK
Publisher: Wise Publications / Music Sales Ltd.
Year: 1995: **ISBN-10:** 0711953767
Pages: 96: **Price:** [?]
Description: Paperback with color pictorial wrappers, 9" x 12". Note: Transcriptions to the songs of *Legend*.

Title: *Legend: the best of Bob Marley and the Wailers*
Author: N/A
Place of Publication: Milwaukee, Wis., U.S.
Publisher: Hal Leonard Corporation
Year: 1995: **ISBN-10:** 0793536987
Pages: 96: **Price:** $19.95
Description: Paperback with color pictorial wrappers, 9" x 12". Note: Transcriptions to the songs of *Legend*.

Title: *Bob Marley: Songs of Freedom*
Author: N/A
Place of Publication: Milwaukee, Wis., U.S.
Publisher: Hal Leonard Corporation
Year: 1992: **ISBN-10:** 0793516846
Pages: 215: **Price:** $24.95 U.S.
Description: Paperback with pictorial wrappers, 9" x 12". Note: Transcriptions to the songs of *Songs of Freedom*.

Title: *Bob Marley: Songs of Freedom*
Author: N/A
Place of Publication: London, UK
Publisher: Wise Publications
Year: 1995: **ISBN-10:** 0711953759
Pages: 215: **Price:** [?]
Description: Paperback with color pictorial wrappers, 9" x 12". Note: Transcriptions to the songs of *Songs of Freedom*.

Title: *The Concise Bob Marley: The Music & Complete Lyrics for 35 Classic Marley Songs*
Author: Compiled by Peter Evans
Place of Publication: London, UK
Publisher: Wise Publications
Year: 1996: **ISBN-10:** 0711951993
Pages: 125: **Price:** None Listed
Description: Paperback with color pictorial wrappers, 6.75" x 9.75". Note: Lyrics and transcriptions to 35 classic songs.

Title: *Natural Mystic: The Legend Lives on- Bob Marley and the Wailers*
Author: N/A
Place of Publication: Milwaukee, Wis., U.S.
Publisher: Hal Leonard Corporation
Year: 1996: **ISBN-10:** 0793551528
Pages: 104: **Price:** $14.95 U.S.
Description: Paperback with color pictorial wrappers, 9" x 12". Note: Transcriptions to the songs of *Natural Mystic*.

Title: *Bob Marley and the Wailers*
Author: N/A
Place of Publication: Paris, France
Publisher: ID Music
Year: 1996: **ISBN-13:** 3553301008048
Pages: [?]: **Price:** [?]
Description: Paperback with color pictorial wrappers, 9" x 12". Note: Lyrics and guitar tablature

Title: *Play Guitar with Bob Marley*
Author: Jason Manger
Place of Publication: London, UK
Publisher: Music Sales Ltd
Year: 1997: **ISBN-10:** 0711958238
Pages: 64: **Price:** [?]
Description: Paperback with color pictorial wrappers, 9" x 12". Note: Transcriptions to seven classic Marley songs. Comes with a CD of backing tracks to play along with.

Title: *Bob Marley and the Wailers*
Author: N/A
Place of Publication: Paris, France
Publisher: ID Music / EMF
Year: 1997: **ISBN-13:** 5020679112656
Pages: 48: **Price:** [?]
Description: Paperback with color pictorial wrappers, 9" x 12". Note: Lyrics and guitar tablature. Transcriptions to 18 songs including *I Shot the Sheriff*, *Natural Mystic* and *Africa Unite*.

Title: *The Best of Bob Marley: Easy Guitar*
Author: N/A
Place of Publication: Milwaukee, Wis., U.S.
Publisher: Hal Leonard Corporation
Year: 1998: **ISBN-10:** 079359412x
Pages: 96: **Price:** $12.95 U.S.
Description: Paperback with color pictorial wrappers, 9" x 12". Note: Transcriptions to 45 songs.

Title: *Bob Marley: The Chord Songbook*
Author(s): Compiled by Nick Crispin and music arranged by Rikky Rooksby
Place of Publication: London, UK
Publisher: Wise Publications
Year: 1999: **ISBN-10:** 0711978328
Pages: 48: **Price:** None Listed
Description: Paperback with color pictorial wrappers, 6.75" x 9.75". Note: Transcriptions to 19 songs.

Title: Acoustic Reggae
Author: Tetsuya Fujita
Place of Publication: Tokyo, Japan
Publisher: Shinko Music Entertainment
Year: 1999: **ISBN-13:** 9784401154012
Pages: 95: **Price:** [?]
Description: Paperback with color pictorial wrappers, 10.25" x 12". Note: Japanese music book with transcriptions to several reggae songs.

Title: *Bob Marley +Best reggae songs by best reggae artist of our time*
Author: N/A
Place of Publication: London, UK
Publisher: Wise Publications
Year: 2000: **ISBN-10:** 071198557x
Pages: 64: **Price:** [?]
Description: Paperback with color pictorial wrappers, 9" x 12". Note: Guitar tablature to several Marley songs.

Title: *Complete Lyrics of Bob Marley: Songs of Freedom*
Author: Lyrics transcribed by Harry Hawke
Place of Publication: London, UK
Publisher: Omnibus Press
Year: 2001: **ISBN-10:** 0711986703
Pages: 191: **Price:** £12.99 UK
Description: Paperback with color pictorial wrappers, 6.75" x 9.75". Note: Lyric transcriptions to 118 songs. Additional working cover that was never used shown below.

Title: *One Love: The Very Best of Bob Marley & The Wailers*
Author: N/A
Place of Publication: London, UK
Publisher: Wise Publications
Year: 2001: **ISBN-10:** 0711991278
Pages: 128: **Price:** [?]
Description: Paperback with color pictorial wrappers, 9" x 12". Note: Transcriptions to the songs of *One Love: The Very Best of Bob Marley & The Wailers*.

Title: *One Love: The Very Best of Bob Marley & The Wailers*
Author: N/A
Place of Publication: Milwaukee, Wis., U.S.
Publisher: Hal Leonard Corporation
Year: 2002: **ISBN-10:** 063404172x
Pages: 136: **Price:** [?]
Description: Paperback with color pictorial wrappers, 9" x 12". Note: Transcriptions to the songs of *One Love: The Very Best of Bob Marley & The Wailers*.

Title: *One Love: The Very Best of Bob Marley & The Wailers*
Author: N/A
Place of Publication: Milwaukee, Wis., U.S.
Publisher: Hal Leonard Corporation
Year: 2002: **ISBN-10:** 0634041711
Pages: 120: **Price:** [?]
Description: Paperback with color pictorial wrappers, 9" x 12". Note: Transcriptions to the songs of *One Love: The Very Best of Bob Marley & The Wailers*.

Title: *The Essential Bob Marley*
Author: N/A
Place of Publication: Milwaukee, Wis., U.S.
Publisher: Hal Leonard Corporation
Year: 2003: **ISBN-10:** 0634047396
Pages: 80: **Price:** [?]
Description: Paperback with color pictorial wrappers, 9" x 12". Note: Transcriptions to 21 classic songs.

Title: *Bob Marley: Los mejores temas para tocar y cantar*
Author: Transcriptions by Daniel Curto
Place of Publication: Buenos Aires, Argentina
Publisher: Ricordi Americana S.A.E.C.
Year: 2004: **ISBN-10:** 9502202880
Pages: 33: **Price:** None Listed
Description: Paperback with color pictorial wrappers, 6" x 8.5". Note: Transcriptions to 19 songs.

Title: *The Very Best of Bob Marley*
Author: N/A
Place of Publication: Milwaukee, Wis., U.S.
Publisher: Hal Leonard Corporation
Year: 2005: **ISBN-10:** 063404740x
Pages: 56: **Price:** [?]
Description: Paperback with color pictorial wrappers, 9" x 12". Note: Transcriptions to 12 songs. Part of the 'Strum It Guitar' series.

Title: *Africa Unite: Il Sogno di Bob Marley*
Author(s): Alberto Castelli and Gullotta M. Carla
Place of Publication: Italy
Publisher: Arcana
Year: 2005: **ISBN-10:** 8879663976
Pages: 185: **Price:** [?]
Description: Paperback with color pictorial wrappers. Note: Title translation: The Dream of Bob Marley. The authors follow Marley's footsteps from Jamaica to Africa and back to Jamaica. A tribute book to the most important musical figure of the twentieth century. Should not be in the music section but rather in the Non English biographies section.

Title: *Bob Marley: Complete Chord Songbook*
Author(s): Compiled by Nick Crispin and music arranged by Rikki Rooksby
Place of Publication: London, UK
Publisher: Wise Publications
Year: 2005: **ISBN-10:** 0711988501
Pages: 272: **Price:** None Listed
Description: Paperback with color pictorial wrappers, 6.75" x 9.75". Note: Transcriptions to 124 songs. The only music book a guitarist would need on a deserted island. Note the curious addition of a Parental Advisory Explicit Lyrics stamp. The stamp is printed on the cover.

Title: *Bob Marley & The Wailers: Super Best*
Author: N/A
Place of Publication: Japan
Publisher: Doremi Music Publishers
Year: 2006: **ISBN-10:** 4285107012
Pages: 156: **Price:** [?]
Description: Paperback with pictorial wrappers, 8.25" x 10.75". Note: Japanese music book with transcriptions to eleven classic Marley songs.

Title: *Bob Marley: Bass Collection*
Author: Music transcriptions by Chris Kringel
Place of Publication: Milwaukee, Wis., U.S.
Publisher: Hal Leonard Corporation
Year: 2007: **ISBN-10:** 063404737x
Pages: 111: **Price:** $17.95 U.S.
Description: Paperback with color pictorial wrappers, 9" x 12". Note: Bass transcriptions to 19 classic Marley songs. Marley's bass player Aston Barrett is considered by many to be the best reggae bass player in the world. His bass lines form the melody and foundation to Bob's timeless songs.

Title: *Bob Marley: The Little Black Songbook*
Author: N/A
Place of Publication: London, UK
Publisher: Wise Publications
Year: 2007: **ISBN-10:** 1846099951
Pages: 192: **Price:** [?]
Description: Paperback with pictorial wrappers, 4.5" x 7.5". Note: Lyrics and music transcriptions to over 80 Marley songs.

Title: *Bob Marley: 4-Chord Songbook*
Author: N/A
Place of Publication: London, UK
Publisher: Wise Publications
Year: 2007: **ISBN 10:** 1846098211
Pages: 48: **Price:** [?]
Description: Paperback with color pictorial wrappers. Note: 29 Marley songs arranged using the same four chords.

Books with Bob on the Cover

Yes, people do judge a book by its cover! Not all books that feature Bob on the cover are devoted to him or his music. Being one of the most recognizable images in the world it should come as no surprise that there are books that use his image on the cover solely to catch the attention of would be buyers. The books listed in this section are just a small sample of the books out there with Bob on the cover. The reason I have included this section is to show the uniqueness of some books that feature Bob on the cover but are not devoted to him. Most are general reggae books or books about Rastafari while several are album guide books.

Color promo card for Rasta Heart, One Love Press 2001
4" x 6"

Title: *Chart Toppers annual 1979*
Author: N/A
Place of Publication: Manchester, UK
Publisher: World Distributers
Year: 1979: **SBN-9:** 723504784
Pages: 64: **Price:** £1.50 UK
Description: Hardcover in color pictorial boards, 8" x 10.75". Note: A review of the 1979 top musical acts.

Title: *Reggae Pur Sang: Musique et Culture de la Jamaique*
Author(s): Stephen Davis and Peter Simon
Place of Publication: France
Publisher: Albin Michel
Year: 1981: **ISBN-10:** 2226010181
Pages: 175: **Price:** [?]
Description: Paperback with color pictorial wrappers. Note: French edition of Davis and Simon's groundbreaking reggae book. This book has two English editions. It is a highly recommended book along with its cousin *Reggae International*.

Title: *les Racines du Reggae: Evolution De La Musique Populaire Jamaiquaine*
Author: Sebastian Clarke
Place of Publication: France
Publisher: Editions Caribeennes
Year: 1981: **ISBN-10:** 2903033269
Pages: [?]: **Price:** [?]
Description: Note: An early French reggae book. Second printing by L'Harmattan in 2000. Title translation: Roots of Reggae: The Evolution of Popular Jamaican Music.

Title: *Reggae: die kings aus Kingstontown*
Author: Ulrich Hoppe
Place of Publication: Munich, Germany
Publisher: Wilhelm Heyne Verlag
Year: 1981: **ISBN-10:** 3453800508
Pages: 203: **Price:** [?]
Description: Paperback with color pictorial wrappers, 7" x 10". Note: Title Translation: The Kings of Kingstontown. A German look at the major figures of reggae.

Title: *Reggae: Deep Roots Music*
Author(s): Howard Johnson and Jim Pines
Place of Publication: New York, U.S. and London, UK
Publisher: Proteus Publisher Co.; Proteus Books Ltd.
Year: 1982: **ISBN 10:** 0862761190 (HC) 0862761174 (PB)
Pages: 127: **Price:** £5.95 UK; $10.95 U.S. (PB)
Description: Paperback with color pictorial wrappers, 7.75" x 10.75". Note: Released in association with Channel 4 television UK. It tells the story of Jamaica, reggae music and important figures such as Marcus Garvey.

Title: *Aux Sources Du Reggae*
Author: Denis Constant
Place of Publication: France
Publisher: Editions Parenthesis
Year: 1982: **ISBN-10:** 2863640143
Pages: 155: **Price:** [?]
Description: Paperback with pictorial wrappers, 6" x 9.5". Note: An early book about reggae. It was an early source of reggae information.

Title: *Jamaican Music*
Author: Michael Burnett
Place of Publication: Oxford, UK
Publisher: Oxford University Press
Year: 1982, 1984 (with corrections), 1986, 1987, 1992, 1994, 1996, 1998: **ISBN-10:** 0193213338
Pages: 48: **Price:** None Listed
Description: Paperback with color pictorial wrappers, 9.75" x 7.5". Note: A history of Jamaican music accompanied by music transcriptions, black and white photos and pictures of Jamaican instruments. 1998 edition shown with Marley and the I-Threes on the cover.

Title: *Reggae and Latin Pop: Hot Sauces*
Author: Billy Bergman
Place of Publication: Dorset, UK
Publisher: Blandford Press
Year: 1985: **ISBN-10:** 0713715528
Pages: 143 : **Price:** None Listed
Description: Paperback with color pictorial wrappers, 7" x 10". Note: A look at Latin and Caribbean music and how it relates to the current music scene.

Title: *The Reggae Files: A Book of Interviews*
Author: Gordon C
Place of Publication: London, UK
Publisher: Hansib Publishing Ltd.
Year: 1988: **ISBN-10:** 1870518039
Pages: 114: **Price:** £6.95 UK
Description: Paperback with color pictorial wrappers, 7" x 9.5". Note: As the title states, this is a book of interviews the author had with several reggae musicians including Bob Marley.

Title: *Twenty names in Pop Music*
Author: Andrew Langley
Place of Publication: Long Island, NY, U.S.
Publisher: Marshall Cavendish Corporation
Year: 1988: **ISBN-10:** 0863079660
Pages: 48: **Price:** None Listed
Description: Hardcover with color boards, 8" x 10". Note: Short biographies on 20 popular musicians. Marley's page has color illustrations and a color photo of him on stage.

Title: *The Guinness Who's Who Of Reggae*
Author: Editor and designer Colin Larkin
Place of Publication: Middlesex, UK
Publisher: Guinness Publishing Ltd.
Year: 1984: **ISBN-10:** 0851127347
Pages: 318: **Price:** £13.99 UK
Description: Paperback with color pictorial wrappers, 6.75" x 9.25". Note: A guide to most of the major and not so major reggae stars. Includes artist's discographies with ratings. Also published in a hardcover edition. Illustrated with several black and white photos. A nice book to own.

Title: *Rasta Cruz: a Reading Coloring Book-Reggae, Culture, Bob Marley*
Author: None
Place of Publication: Santa Cruz, Calif., U.S.
Publisher: Rasta Cruz Publishers
Year: 1992: **ISBN-10:** None
Pages: 24: **Price:** None Listed
Description: Paperback with pictorial wrappers, 8.5" x 11". Note: A coloring book for the kids. All pictures are reggae related and several are of Brother Bob.

Title: *Reggae on CD: The Essential Guide*
Author: Lloyd Bradley
Place of Publication: London, UK
Publisher: Kyle Cathie Limited
Year: 1996: **ISBN-10:** 1856261778
Pages: 368: **Price:** £9.99 UK
Description: Paperback with color pictorial wrappers, 5" x 7.75". Note: A guide to hundreds of essential reggae CDs.

Title: *Reggae: The Rough Guide*
Author: Steve Barrow and Peter Dalton
Place of Publication: London, UK
Publisher: Rough Guides Ltd.
Year: 1997: **ISBN-10:** 1858282470
Pages: 395: **Price:** £12.99 UK; $27.95 Australia; $25.99 Canada; $19.95 U.S.
Description: First edition, Paperback with color pictorial wrappers, 6.5" x 9.25". Note: A comprehensive guide to numerous reggae albums with ratings. Illustrated with photos and album covers.

Title: *Reggae Rastafarians Revolution: Jamaican Music from Ska to Dub*
Author: Chris Potash
Place of Publication: New York, U.S.
Publisher: Schirmer Books
Year: 1997: **ISBN-10:** 0028647289
Pages: 290: **Price:** $22.00 U.S.
Description: Hardcover. Note: The story of Jamaican music told through fanzines, various academic forums and Caribbean newspapers. Not sure if this is indeed the cover of a hardcover edition or an early title and cover that was not used. I have been unable to locate a hardcover edition. I'm going to assume it's an early cover and title that were never used.

Title: *Reggae, Rasta, Revolution: jamaican music from ska to dub*
Author: Chris Potash
Place of Publication: New York, U.S.
Publisher: Schirmer Books
Year: 1997: **ISBN-10:** 0028647289
Pages: 290: **Price:** $22.00 U.S.
Description: Paperback with color pictorial wrappers, 6" x 9". Note: The story of Jamaican music told through fanzines, various academic forums and Caribbean newspapers.

Title: *Reggae Routes: The Story of Jamaican Music*
Author(s): Kevin O'Brian Chang and Wayne Chen
Place of Publication: Philadelphia, U.S.
Publisher: Temple University Press
Year: 1998: **ISBN-10:** 1566396298
Pages: 246: **Price:** None Listed
Description: Paperback with color pictorial wrappers, 6.75" x 9.25". Note: Each stage of Jamaican music is documented from a Jamaican perspective. Reggae Routes profiles artists, producers and recordings that form the foundation of reggae music. Illustrated with black and white photos.

Title: *Reggae Disc Guide*
Author: [?]
Place of Publication: Japan
Publisher: [?]
Year: 1998: **ISBN:** [?]
Pages: 214: **Price:** [?]
Description: Note: A Japanese guide to hundreds of reggae albums.

Title: A Century of Pop: A Hundred Years of Music that Changed the World-From Vaudeville to Rock, Big Band to Techno
Author: Hugh Gregory
Place of Publication: Chicago, Ill., U.S.
Publisher: Chicago Review Press / ACapella Books
Year: 1998: **ISBN-10:** 1556523386
Pages: 252: **Price:** [?]
Description: Paperback with color pictorial wrapper. Note: A look back at the history and roots of music and how they relate to current popular music. Illustrated with hundreds of pictures.

Title: *Reggae*
Author: Bob Brunning
Place of Publication: Lincolnwood, Ill., U.S.
Publisher: Peter Bedrick Books
Year: 1999: **ISBN-10:** 0872265773
Pages: 32: **Price:** $15.95 U.S.
Description: Hardcover with color pictorial boards, 9.5" x 11.5". Note: Short biographies about several of the most popular reggae artists. Illustrated with several color photos. Part of the 'Sound Trackers' music series.

Title: *On Racial Frontiers: The New Culture of Frederick Douglass, Ralph Ellison, and Bob Marley*
Author: Gregory Stephens
Place of Publication: Cambridge, UK
Publisher: The Press Syndicate of the University of Cambridge
Year: 1999: **ISBN-10:** 052164352x (HC); 0521643937 (PB)
Pages: 329: **Price:** None Listed
Description: Hardcover, paperback with color pictorial wrappers, 6" x 9". Note: A scholarly look at racial situations. Includes a fascinating section on Marcus Garvey and is illustrated with black and white photos.

Title: *the black chord*
Author(s): Vivien Goldman and David Corio (Foreword by Isaac Hayes)
Place of Publication: New York, U.S.
Publisher: Universe Publishing
Year: 1999: **ISBN-10:** 078930337x (HC); 0789303752 (PB)
Pages: 176: **Price:** $45.00 U.S.; $70.00 Canada (HC) / $29.95 U.S.; $46.50 Canada (PB)
Description: Hardcover, full black boards, lettered in yellow and silver, in color pictorial dust jacket, 8.75" x 11.5". Paperback with color pictorial wrappers, 8.5" x 11" Note: A black and white photo book accompanied by text about the subjects which range from Marley to B.B. King. It is heavy on the reggae photos.

Title: *Natural Mysticism Towards a new reggae aesthetic*
Author: Kwame Dawes
Place of Publication: Leeds, UK
Publisher: Peepal Tree Press
Year: 1999: **ISBN-10:** 1900715228
Pages: 280: **Price:** £12.99 UK
Description: Paperback with color pictorial wrappers, 5.5" x 8". Note: A look at how reggae music helped define the author while also taking a look at the rise of reggae in the 1970s and the writings of Caribbean authors.

Title: *Reggae: 100 Essential CDs The Rough Guide*
Author(s): Steve Barrow and Peter Dalton
Place of Publication: London, UK
Publisher: Rough Guides Ltd.
Year: 1999: **ISBN-10:** 1858285674
Pages: 208: **Price:** £5.00 UK; $12.99 Canada; $8.95 U.S.
Description: Paperback with color pictorial wrappers, 4" x 5.5". Note: A guide to 100 essential reggae CDs. Illustrated with album covers.

Title: *Le Guide Du Rastaman: Le Movement Rastafari Jamaiquain*
Author: Etienne T. Babagbeto
Place of Publication: France
Publisher: Les Editions Inconeg
Year: 2000: **ISBN-10:** 2951410409
Pages: 233: **Price:** [?]
Description: Paperback with color pictorial wrappers, 6" x 8.25". Note: French book about Rastafari.

Title: *Reggae Explosion: The Story of Jamaican Music*
Author(s): Chris Salewicz and Adrian Boot, (Introduction by Chris Blackwell)
Place of Publication: New York, U.S.
Publisher: Harry N. Abrams, Incorporated
Year: 2001: **ISBN-10:** 0810981696
Pages: 224: **Price:** $24.98
Description: Hardcover, full brown cloth, lettered in ivory, in color pictorial dust jacket, 10.5" x 12.25". Note: Informative book about reggae, illustrated with color and black and white photos. This was the only edition that featured Marley on the cover.

Title: Best Reggae Hits
Author: Miki Michizou
Place of Publication: Tokyo, Japan
Publisher: Shinko Music Entertainment
Year: 2001: **ISBN-13:** 9784401732562
Pages: 96: **Price:** [?]
Description: Paperback with color pictorial wrappers. Note: Music transcriptions to 24 reggae songs. Marley songs include: *Is This Love, No Woman, No Cry, Could You Be Loved, One Love (People Get Ready)* and *I Shot the Sheriff.*

Title: *Rasta Heart: A Journey Into One Love*
Author(s): Robert Roskind and Julia Roskind
Place of Publication: Blowing Rock, N.C., U.S.
Publisher: One Love Press
Year: 2001: **ISBN-10:** 1565220749
Pages: 302: **Price:** $14.95 U.S.
Description: Paperback with color pictorial wrappers, 6" x 9". Note: A journey into the Rasta heart of Jamaica by the author and his family. Roskind is on a journey to find the meaning and nature of the 'One Love' that Marley sang about in his songs. During the search we meet several new friends on our way to the One Love summit which was held at 56 Hope Road. A fun and insightful book.

Title: *Reggae Wisdom- Proverbs in Jamaican Music*
Author: Sw.Anand Prahlad
Place of Publication: Jackson, Miss., U.S.
Publisher: University Press of Mississippi
Year: 2001: **ISBN-10:** 1578063205
Pages: 302: **Price:** None Listed
Description: Paperback with color pictorial wrappers, 5.75" x 9". Note: A look at the origins of reggae lyrics and proverbs while using them as a history lesson in Jamaican culture.

Title: *Rastafari In Transition: The Politics Of Cultural Confrontation In Africa And The Caribbean (1966-1988)*
Author: Ikael Tafari, Ph.D (Foreword by Barry Chevannes)
Place of Publication: Chicago, U.S.
Publisher: Frontline Distribution International
Year: 2001: **ISBN-10:** 0948390832
Pages: 360: **Price:** $25.00
Description: Paperback with color pictorial wrappers, 5.5" x 8.5". Note: A look at Rastafari and politricks.

Title: *The Rough Guide To Reggae*
Author(s): Steve Barrow and Peter Dalton
Place of Publication: London, UK
Publisher: Rough Guides Ltd.
Year: 2001: **ISBN-10:** 1858285585
Pages: 475: **Price:** £13.99 UK; $21.95 U.S.; $31.99 Can.
Description: Second edition, paperback with color pictorial wrappers, 6" x 9.25". Note: A comprehensive guide to numerous reggae albums with ratings. Illustrated with photos and album covers. Third edition did not feature Marley on the cover.

Title: *The Rastaman Vibration: Jamaican Culture and More!*
Author: Ras Zuke
Place of Publication: Naples, Fla., U.S.
Publisher: Far-Eye Productions
Year: 2002: **ISBN-10:** 0972063501
Pages: 238: **Price:** $24.99 U.S.
Description: Paperback with color pictorial wrappers, 8.5" x 11". Note: Kind of a hodgepodge of a book, it talks about Rastafari, Marley, dreadlocks and many other things. Includes black and white photos, a section on how to speak Patois, transcriptions to the movie *Rockers* and a Marley interview.

Title: *Reggae & Caribbean Music*
Author: Dave Thompson
Place of Publication: San Francisco, U.S.
Publisher: Back Beat Books
Year: 2002: **ISBN-10:** 0879306556
Pages: 532: **Price:** $24.95 U.S.
Description: Paperback with color pictorial wrappers, 7.5" x 9.25". Note: Reviews and ratings to thousands of reggae albums. Includes short biographies and a few black and white photos.

Title: *Reggae*
Author: Paolo Ferrari
Place of Publication: Florence, Italy
Publisher: Giunti Editore
Year: 2002: **ISBN-10:** 8809025229
Pages: 128: **Price:** 6,90 €
Description: Paperback with color pictorial wrappers. 6" x 8.5". Note: A look at dozens of reggae artists and a sample of their works. Illustrated with color photos.

Title: *Reggae-Lexikon: Rastas, Riddims, Roots & Reggae, Vom Ska Bis Zum Dancehall, Die Musik, Die Aus Jamaike Kam*
Author: Rainer Bratfisch
Place of Publication: Berlin, Germany
Publisher: Schwarzkopf & Schwarzkopf
Year: 2002: **ISBN-10:** 3896022075
Pages: 351: **Price:** [?]
Description: First edition, paperback with color pictorial wrappers. Note: A German guide to all genres of reggae.

Title: *One Love, One Heart: A History of Reggae*
Author: James Haskins
Place of Publication: New York, U.S.
Publisher: Jump at the Sun
Year: 2002: **ISBN-10:** 0786804793
Pages: 138: **Price:** $15.99 U.S.; $22.99 Canada
Description: Hardcover, black quarter board and green boards, lettered in white, in color pictorial dust jacket, 6.25" x 9.5". Note: A history lesson in Jamaica, reggae music and Bob Marley. Illustrated with black and white photos.

Title: *Das grobe Reggae Lexikon: Rastas, Riddims, Roots & Reggae vom Ska Bis Zum Dancehall Die Musik, Die Aus Jamaike Kam*
Author: Rainer Bratfisch
Place of Publication: Berlin, Germany
Publisher: Schwarzkopf & Schwarzkopf
Year: 2003: **ISBN-10:** 3896025163
Pages: 590: **Price:** [?]
Description: Second edition, paperback with color pictorial wrappers, 6.75" x 9.25". Note: A German guide to all genres of reggae.

Title: *The First Rasta: Leonard Howell and the Rose of Rastafarianism*
Author: Helene Lee (Introduction: Stephen Davis)
Place of Publication: Chicago, Ill., U.S.
Publisher: Chicago Review Press, Inc.
Year: 2003: **ISBN 10:** 1566524668 (HC), 1556525583 (PB)
Pages: 306: **Price:** $26.95 (HC) $16.95 (PB) U.S.; $25.95 (PB) Canada
Description: Hardcover, in color pictorial dust jacket and paperback with color pictorial wrappers, 6" x 9". Note: A thrilling and fantastic journey on the search for Leonard Howell and the origins of Rastafari. From the streets of NYC to the hills of Jamaica, Lee does some serious digging.

Title: *Rebel Musics*
Author(s): Daniel Fischlin and Ajay Heble editors
Place of Publication: Montreal, Canada
Publisher: Black Rose Books
Year: 2003: **ISBN-10:** 155164231x (HC) 1551642301 (PB)
Pages: 254: **Price:** $24.99 U.S.; £16.99 UK
Description: Paperback with color pictorial wrappers, 5.75" x 9". Note: A look at many types of music and how that music can create a loud voice. Illustrated with black and white photos.

Title: *Voir Trench Town Et Mourir: Les Annees Bob Marley*
Author: Helene Lee
Place of Publication: Paris, France
Publisher: Flammarion
Year: 2004: **ISBN-10:** 2080684051
Pages: 402: **Price:** 19 €
Description: Paperback with color pictorial wrappers, 7.75" x 9.75". Note: The history of Trench Town and how it influenced Marley's lyrics and attitude. Title translation: See Trench Town and Die: The Years of Bob Marley.

Title: *Reggae Jamaica*
Author: Antoine Giacomoni
Place of Publication: Bologna, Italy
Publisher: Horizon Illimite
Year: 2004: **ISBN-10:** 2847870598
Pages: 144: **Price:** 39,90 €
Description: Hardcover with color pictorial boards, 11" x 11". Note: Italian book about reggae culture. May have also been printed in paperback.

Title: *Dubwise: reasoning from the reggae underground*
Author: Klive Walker
Place of Publication: Toronto, Canada
Publisher: Insomniac Press
Year: 2005: **ISBN-10:** 1894663969
Pages: 292: **Price:** $31.95 Canada; $16.95 U.S.; £9.95 UK; $21.95 Australia
Description: Paperback with color pictorial wrappers, 6" x 9". Note: A nice look at reggae from a Canadian point of view. Includes lots of information about Marley, women in reggae and UK reggae. Illustrated with a few black and white photos.

Title: *Le reggae*
Author: Bruno Blum (Preface: Sly & Robbie)
Place of Publication: Paris, France
Publisher: J'Ai Lu
Year: 2000: **ISBN-10:** 2290348058
Pages: 125: **Price:** 2 €
Description: Paperback with color pictorial wrappers, 5" x 8". Note: A Guide to all phases of reggae music by the very knowledgeable French musician, author and artist Bruno Blum. Includes a discography and several illustrations. Preface is by two of the genres most important riddim duos.

Title: *Rasta Chant: Das Who is Who des Roots-Reggae*
Author: Volker Barsch
Place of Publication: Mainz, Germany
Publisher: Ventil Verlag
Year: 2006: **ISBN-10:** 3931555917
Pages: 268: **Price:** 14,90 €
Description: Paperback with color pictorial wrappers, 6" x 9". Note: A German look at who's who in roots reggae.

Title: *From Garvey to Marley: Rastafari Theology*
Author: Noel Leo Erskine (Foreword by Stephen W. Angell and Anthony Pinn)
Place of Publication: Gainesville, Fla., U.S.
Publisher: University of Florida Press
Year: 2007: **ISBN 10:** 0813028078 (HC); 0813030781 (PB)
Pages: 225: **Price:** $39.95 U.S. (HC); $24.95 U.S. (PB)
Description: Hardcover, in color pictorial dust jacket and paperback with color pictorial wrapper, 6" x 9". Note: A scholarly look at Rastafari.

Title: *Jamaique: Sur la Piste du Reggae*
Author: Bruno Blum text and drawings
Place of Publication: Paris, France
Publisher: Scali
Year: 2007: **ISBN-10:** 2350121720
Pages: 110: **Price:** 36 €
Description: Paperback with color pictorial wrappers, 8" x 9.5". Note: A history lesson in 1970s Jamaican reggae music, Jamaican recording studios, ghetto violence and the beautiful mysticism of the island. Illustrated with the authors own art. Another offering from French reggae authority Bruno Blum.

Title: *The Big Guitar Chord Songbook Reggae*
Author: N/A
Place of Publication: London, UK
Publisher: Omnibus Press
Year: 2007: **ISBN-10:** 184609674x
Pages: 192: **Price:** [?]
Description: Paperback with color pictorial wrappers, 6.75" x 9.5". Note: Transcriptions to over 80 reggae songs by various musicians including Bob Marley & The Wailers.

Title: *His Eminence Abuna Yesehaq Mandefro*
Author: Juliet delia' Ann Wilkinson
Place of Publication: U.S.
Publisher: Author House
Year: 2008: **ISBN-10:** 1434305481
Pages: 88: **Price:** [?]
Description: Paperback with color pictorial wrappers, 6" x 9". Note: The story of the author and her relationship with Abuna Yesehaq Mandefro. Yesehaq was the one who baptized Marley into the Ethiopian Orthodox Church. He also presided over Marley's state funeral in Jamaica.

Title: *Exodus!: L'histoire du retour des Rastafariens en Ethiopie*
Author: Giulia Bonacci
Place of Publication: Paris, France
Publisher: Scali
Year: 2008: **ISBN-10:** 2350122093
Pages: 798: **Price:** [?]
Description: Paperback with color pictorial wrappers, 6" x 9.25". Note: The story of Rasta repatriation to Shashemene land in Ethiopia. Title translation: Exodus: The Story of the Return of Rastafarians in Ethiopia. Shashemene is a plot of land donated to the Rasta and EWF by Emperor Haile Selassie I.

Title: *Das grobe Reggae Lexikon: Rastas, Riddims, Roots & Reggae vom Ska Bis Zum Dancehall Die Musik, Die Aus Jamaike Kam*
Author: Rainer Bratfisch
Place of Publication: Berlin, Germany
Publisher: Schwarzkopf & Schwarzkopf
Year: [?]: **ISBN-10:** 3896025163
Pages: 592: **Price:** 24,90 €
Description: Second printing of second edition, paperback with color pictorial wrappers, 6.5" x 9.25". Note: A German guide to all genres of reggae.

Title: One Drop Drumming: Die Kunst des Reggae-Schlagzeugspiels im Stil von Carlton Barrett
Author: Dengue Felix
Place of Publication: Germany
Publisher: Bosworth Music GmbH
Year: 2008: **SBN-10:** 3865432816
Pages: 64: **Price:** 22,50 €
Description: Paperback with color pictorial wrappers. Note: Title translation: The Art of Reggae Drumming in the Style of Carlton Barrett. Carly Barrett was Marley's drummer for the majority of his career. He is the brother of Aston Barrett, The Wailers bass player. Their story is documented in the *Wailing Blues* book by John Masouri. Comes with a CD.

Title: *keep on running: the story of island records*
Author: Chris Salewicz, editor
Place of Publication: London, UK
Publisher: Universal-Island Records & The Island Trading Company Ltd.
Year: 2009: **ISBN-13:** 9780956191403
Pages: 223: **Price:** £25.00 UK
Description: Hardcover, full red decorated boards, lettered in white and black, in color pictorial dust jacket, 9.75" x 9.75". Note: The complete story of Island Records with lots of info on reggae and Bob Marley. Illustrated with color photos of artists, Chris Blackwell and album covers. Contributions by several authors and photographers.

Color promo post card for The First Rasta, Lawrence Hill Books 2003
6" x 8"

Titles Index

Since so many titles begin with *Bob Marley*, there is a Bob Marley section under **B**. Any title that starts with 'Bob Marley' will be found there.

A
A Century of Pop, 141
Acoustic Reggae, 127
Africa Unite, 130
A Rasta's Pilgrimage, 62
Aux Sources Du Reggae, 136

B
Before The Legend, 34, 38, 117
Best Reggae Hits, 143
Best of Bob Marley, The (Song), 126
Big Guitar Chord Songbook, The, 150
Black Chord, The, 142
Bob Marley & Jamaica (Japan), 104
Book of Exodus, The, 34
Boy From Nine Miles, The. 73

Bob Marley Titles:
Bob Marley (Greek), 95
Bob Marley (K. Beggs), 10
Bob Marley (S. Bennett), 22, 23
Bob Marley (M. Bronson), 16, 107, 113
Bob Marley (S. Davis), 4, 5, 6, 8, 11, 12, 13, 15, 17, 35, 38, 84, 86, 87, 105, 109
Bob Marley (S. Dolan),23
Bob Marley (F. Dordor), 86, 88, 90
Bob Marley (M. Evert), 91
Bob Marley (M. Gilfoyle), 20, 25
Bob Marley (M. Gomez) 110
Bob Marley (A. Martinez), 114
Bob Marley (C. May), 9, 10
Bob Marley (El-Fers), 96
Bob Marley (R. Monpierre), 72
Bob Marley (C. Quilici), 80
Bob Marley (G. Steckles), 39, 40
Bob Marley (M. Vasquez), 113
Bob Marley (M. Ward), 15, 21, 84, 118
Bob Marley (C. Welch), 18, 21, 118
Bob Marley & The Wailers (J. Green), 42
Bob Marley & The Wailers (M. Cotto), 99
Bob Marley & The Wailers (Song), 121, 125, 126
A Bibliography, 9, 42
A Biography, 37
A Book of Postcards, 61
A Life, 40
A Musical Drama, 42
An Independent Story in Words & Pictures, 8
An Intimate Portrait by His Mother, 21, 22, 27
A Rebel Life. 63, 65, 66
A Tear out Photo Book, 61
Bass Collection, 131
Begirunea, Maitasuna eta askatasuna, 79
Best of Special Guitare Tabs, 122
Best Reggae Songs, 127
Black Americans of Achievement, 23, 36
Canciones, 114
Canzoni, 97, 99, 100, 101, 118
Chord Songbook, The, 127
Collector (D. Sloane), 89
Complete Chord Songbook, 131
Complete Guide to His Music, 49, 54, 106, 109
Complete Guide to the Music of BM, 45
Conquering Lion of Reggae, 15, 17, 35, 39
De A-Z, 86, 88
Definitive Discography, The, 44, 50
Den Tredje Verdens Superstar, 110
Der Ausnahmepoet, 48
Die Legende der Wailers, 74
El Profeta del Reggae, 79
En Bandes Dessinees, 76
Herald of the Postcolonial World, 36, 37
His Musical Legacy, 51, 52, 53
Icon, 66
Illustrated Disco/Biography, 45
Il Mito del Reggae, 100
In Eighenten Worten, 93
In His Own Words, 16, 29, 93, 106, 117
In This life, 103
Island Prophet, 25
I testi originali con traduzione regionata, 100
File, The BM, 108
4-Chord Songbook, 132
Grande Personajes, 110
Kenzi Sozleriyle, 115
Konig des Reggae, 92
L' Africain, 55
L' Integrale, 47, 52
La Legende, 88
La Legende des Wailers, 73, 74
La Legende du Lion, 75
La Star Legendaire du Reggae, 73

Legend (F. de Vitis), 98
Legend (Song), 123
Legende Rasta, 85, 118
Le Prophete Spiritual, 90
Le Rasta, 83
Le Reggae & Les Rastas, 87
L'historre de BM (E.Frank), 85
Little Black Songbook, 132
Life of a Musical Legend, The, 74, 75, 76
Lives: Rasta, Reggae & Resistance, 4
Los Mejores temas para tocar y cantar music, 130
Lyrical Genius, 48, 54
Man and His Music, The, 29
Mies, Musiikki & Mystiika, 83
Musicien Poete Militant Rasta Prophete, 85
Music Myth & The Rastas, 3
My Son, 27
Mythos, Musik & Rastas, 92
One Love, One Heart (Japan), 108
Pop Rock, 38
Por ele Mesmo, 81
Positive Vibration, 112
Rastaman Vibration (Music), 121
Rasta Reggae, 95
Rasta Reggae Rebellion, 90
Rasta Vision of a New World, 42
Reader, The BM, 30
Rebell und Botschaffer des reggae, 91
Rebel With a Cause, 59, 60
Reggae (D. Abel), 113
Reggae (B. Eldem), 116
Reggae King of the World, 7, 12, 17, 24, 26, 118
Reggae Rastafari-ein kurzes schnelles leben, 91
Reggae, Ska, Pop, Rock, 112
Remembered, 42
Roots of Reggae, The, 3
Sa vie les fans Anecdotes Chansons, 113
Sipur Hayav, 97
Songs of African Redemption, 47, 56
Songs of Freedom (Bio), 19, 24, 56, 85, 105, 110, 118
Songs of Freedom (Song), 123, 124
Soul Rebel (M. Sheridan), 46
Soul Rebel (D. Burnett), 67, 68
Soul Rebel-Natural Mystic, 59, 118, 163
Soul Survivor (M. Sheridan), 46
Spirit Dancer, 58, 60, 61, 65
Story, The BM, 9
Story und Songs Kompakt, 49
Su Legado Musical, 53
Super Best (Music), 131
Tale of the Tuff Gong, 71, 72
Talkin' Blues, 82
Talking, 29
Tesori e Ricordi, 103
They Died Too Young, 20, 25
Tribute, 104
Una Vita di Fuoco, 101
Un Rebelle, un Sage, 66
Untold Story, The, 41
Wailing Soul, The, 47

C
Catch a Fire: The Life of Bob Marley, 5, 6, 7, 10, 11, 13, 14, 18, 22, 24, 25, 26, 33, 82, 91, 93, 101, 107, 111, 115
Chart Toppers, 135
Coluleur Reggae, 63
Color Reggae, 63
Complete Guide to the Music of BM, 49
Complete Lyrics of BM, 128
Concise Bob Marley, 124

D
Definitive Discography, The, 44, 50
Dev. Of JA Pop Music, 4
Dictionnaire des Chansons de BM, 51
Do The Reggae, 92
Dubwise, 148
Dunia Dalam Ganja, 96

E
Efsanehin Dogusu, 117
El Codigo BM, 111
Essential BM (Song), 129
Exodus BMW Exile 1977, 36, 89, 94, 102
Exodus! L'histoire du retour des Rastafariens en Ethiopie, 151

F
Falsata Mirindimo, 116
56 Thoughts from Hope Rd., 27
First Rasta, The, 147, 152
From Garvey to Marley, 149

G
Get up! Stand Up! Diary of a Reggaeophile, 27
Guia Musical de BM, 54
Guinness Who's Who of Reggae, 138
Guns & Ganja, 28

H
His Eminence Abuna Yesehaq, 150

I
I & I BM, 70, 76
J
Jamaican Music, 137
Jamaique: Sur la Piste du Reggae, 150
Joseph: A Rasta Reggae Fable, 13, 14, 35
Junto a los Rios de bibliona de BM, 112
K
Keep on Running, 152
L
La Legende de BM. 72
L'alibrary bindingum du Souvenir, 118
L'integrale BM, 52
La Storia dietro ogni Canzone di BM, 101
Le Canzoni de BM, 101
Le Guide du Rastaman, 143
Le Lecrime di BM, 102
Lejonets Trihetssang, 116
Les Racines du Reggae, 135
Le Reggae, 149
M
Marley and Me. 18. 20. 26. 106
Marley: Illustrated Legend 45-81, 17, 21, 107
Marley Journal, 41
Marley: Lejonets Trihetssang, 116
Marley Legend, 34, 35, 88, 94, 103, 108
Marley (Music Icons), 40
Metaphysical Interpretations of BM's Exodus, 48
N
Natural Mystic (Song), 124
Natural Mysticism, 142
No Woman No Cry, The Life of BM, 3

All Editions of Rita Marley's No Woman No Cry are Listed below
No Woman No Cry: My Life with BM (UK and U.S.), 30, 31, 32, 33
H Zoh Moy Me Ton BM (Greece), 96
Ile hayatim (Turkey), 117
Japan edition, 109
La Mia Vita Con BM (Italy), 102
Ma vie avec BM (France), 87
Mein Leben Mit BM (Germany), 94
Minha vida con BM (Brazil), 81
Mi vida junto a BM (Spain), 78, 115
Russian edition, 111
Sipur Hayav (Israel), 97

O
Ohen v Dlanich Zivot BM, 82
One Drop Drumming (**Carly Barrett**), 151
One Love: Life with BMW, 28, 58
One Love, Best of, 128, 129
One Love, One Heart, 146
On Racial Frontiers, 141
P
Peter Tosh: el ministro del Reggae, 82
Peter Tosh: Canzoni, 97
Philosophy of BM, The, 12
Play Guitar with BM, 125
Q
Queimando Tudo, 81
R
Rastafaris: La Mistica de BM, 79
Rastafari in Transition, 144
Rasta Chant, 149
Rasta Cruz, 138
Rasta Heart, 134, 144
Rastaman Vibration, The, 121, 145
Rasta Marley, 103
Rebel Music (K. Simon), 64, 65
Rebel Musics, 147
Reggae (C. Morrow), 62
Reggae (F. Paolo), 146
Reggae & Caribbean Music, 145
Reggae & Latin Pop, 137
Reggae: Da BM ai police…, 98
Reggae: Deep Roots Music, 136
Reggae: die Kings aus Kingstontown, 136
Reggae Disc Guide, 140
Reggae Explosion, 143
Reggae Files, The, 137
Reggae Jamaica, 148
Reggae Lexikon, 146, 147, 151
Reggae Marley, 98, 99
Reggae on CD, 139
Reggae 100 Essential CDs, 142
Reggae Rastafarians Revolution, 139
Reggae Rasta Revolution, 140
Reggae Rocks the World, 122
Reggae Routes, 140
Reggae Poet, 40
Reggae Pur Sang, 135
Reggae Rebel: La Vie de BM, 71
Reggae Rebel: Life of Peter Tosh, 29
Reggae Scrapbook, 67
Reggae (Sound Trackers), 141
Reggae Wisdom, 144

Robert Nesta Marley 10 Greatest Hits, 122
Rock Lives, 42
Rough Guide, Reggae, 139, 142, 145
S
60 Visions, 32
So Much Things to Say, 20
Songs of the Lion, 104
Stir it Up, 62
Super Rock Guide, 106
Sur La Route avec BM, 89
Sur Le Chemin de Retour, 80
T
Talking, 29
The Bob Marley Reader, 30

The Bob Marley Story (Ace), 9
Three Little Birds, 74
Trenchtown Reggae, 115
Trench Town Seben und Sterben, 93
Twenty Names in Pop Music, 138
V
Very Best of BM, 130
Vibes From BM, 105
Visual Music, 66
Voir Trench Town, 148
W
Wailing Blues (**Aston Barrett**), 39
World of Reggae, The, 64, 120
Words & Music of BM, The, 37

Index People

A
Abel, David F., 113
Achilli, Allesandro, 101
Adduci, Giuseppe, 98
Albot, Olivier, 84, 86, 87
Aldred, Jim, 42
Amlak, Issachar ye, 48
Andriopouku, Dimitra, 95
Angel, Stephen W., 149
Aoki, Makoto, 107
Archbold, Sergio Santana, 82
Arnold, Anthony, 101
Assante, Ernesto, 97, 98
B
Babagbeto, Etienne, 143
Baggs, Karen, 10
Barrow, Steve, 139, 142, 145
Barrett, A, 39, 131 / Barsch, Volker, 149
Barrett, C, 39, 151 / Bennett, Scotty, 22, 23
Bergman, Billy, 137
Bermudez, Dario, 79
Benyon, Peter, 10
Blackwell, Chris, 143, 152
Blum, Bruno, 55, 63, 65, 66, 87, 89, 149, 150
Bolelli, Francom, 98
Bonacci, Giulia, 151
Booker, Cedella, 21, 22, 27, 97
Boot, Adrian, 19, 24, 42, 59, 85, 98, 105, 110, 118, 143

Bordowitz, Hank, 30
Bradley, Lloyd, 139
Bratfisch, Rainer, 146, 147, 151
Brunning, Bob, 141
Bronson, Marsha, 16, 107, 113
Brooks, David, 66
Bunshtain, Gil, 97
Burgos, Sawnie, 79
Burnett, David, 76, 68
Burnett, Michael, 137
C
C, Gordon, 137
Campbell, Horace, 4
Carla, Gullotta M., 130
Castelli, Alberto, 130
Chang, Kevin O'Brian, 140
Chen, Wayne, 140
Chevannes, Barry, 144
Clarke, Sebastian, 42, 135
Clarke, Suzanne, 42
Colan, Gene, 71, 72
Collingwood, Jeremy, 51, 52, 53
Constant, Denis, 136
Cooper, Carolyn, 29
Cordosa, Marco Antonio, 81
Corio, David, 142
Cotto, Massimo, 99, 102
Crampton, Luke, 40
Crispin, Nick, 127, 131

Cumbo, Fikisha, 27
Curto, Daniel, 130
D
D' anna, Andrea, 97
Dalrymple, Henderson, 3, 90, 92, 95
Dalton, Peter, 139, 142, 145
Damn, Ursula, 93
Daniel, G. Mahougnon David, 80
Davis, Stephen, 4, 5, 6, 8, 11, 12, 13, 15, 17, 35, 39, 84, 86, 87, 105, 109, 135
Dawes, Kwame, 48, 54, 142, 147
Debritto, Abel, 115
Dedekind, Henning, 94
Delhaye, Tao, 55
De Vitas, Francesco, 98
Diago, Merce, 115
Dolan, Sean, 23
Dordor, Francis, 85, 86, 88, 90
Dzhous, Khetti, 111
E
Edward, Winsome, 42
Eldem, Burak, 116
El-Fers, Mohamed, 96
Erskine, Noel, 149
Evans, Peter, 124
Evert, Manfred, 91
F
Farley, Christopher John, 34, 38, 117
Ferrari, Paolo, 146
Felix, Dengue, 151
Fischlin, Daniel, 147
Flack, Roberta, 27
Fox, Mariah, 73, 74
Frank, Erik, 85
Fujita, Tetsuya, 127
G
Gallo, Armando, 98
Garlan, Judy, 33
Garrick, Neville, 62
Giacomoni, Antoine, 148
Gilfoyle, Millie, 20, 25
Golaszewski, Slawomir, 111
Goldman, Vivien, 34, 59, 118, 142
Gomez, Marlene, 110
Goralski, Maciej, 111
Gottlieb, Kim, 121
Green, Jonathan, 42
Gregory, Hugh, 141
Grompi, Marco, 100, 101, 118
Guilliminot, Herve, 86, 88

Gurdemir, Ela, 117
H
Hahn, Roland, 93
Hall, Charles E., 71, 72
Hannah, Barbara Makeda Blake, 13, 14, 35
Harris, Heather, 121
Hartwig, Astrid, 118
Haskins, James, 146
Hausman, Gerald, 27, 73, 74
Hawke, Harry, 49, 54, 109, 128
Hayes, Isaac, 142
Hazime, Ooishi, 54, 109
Heble, Ajay, 147
Henke, James, 34, 35, 88, 94, 103, 108
Henry, Mike, 18, 20, 26, 28, 106
Hernandez, David Agusti, 115
Herre, Max, 93
Heuff, Liidia, 42
Hoppe, Ulrich, 136
Hussey, Dermott, 7, 8, 12, 17, 24, 26, 104, 118
I
Ibeh, Vitalis, 12
Ingham, Toby, 61
Irazusta, Josetxo Mintegi, 112
Irungu, James, 42
J
Jaffe, Lee, 28, 59
Jarosinski, Arthur, 111
Jeffrey, Gary, 74, 75, 76
Johnson, Howard, 136
Jones, Hettie, 30, 31, 32, 33, 81, 87, 93, 96, 102, 109, 111, 115, 117
K
Kanzi, Hirota, 108
Khalik, Abdul, 96
Kopp, Robert, 92
Kosmos, Kari, 83
Kringel, Chris, 131
L
Langley, Andrew, 138
Larkin, Colin, 138
Lazell, Barry, 17, 21, 107
Lee, Helene, 84, 86, 87, 93, 115, 147, 148
Levi, Makeda, 13, 14, 35
Lindberg, Christer, 116
Litvin, Annie, 94
Lohmann, Uwe, 74
Lu, Prof, 73
Lucini, Gianni, 100

M
Magege, Augustos S., 116
Maillot, Elodie, 51
Manger, Jason, 125
Marley, Bob, 27, 32, 103
Marley, Cedella, 27, 32, 73, 74
Marley, Cedella Booker, 21, 22, 27, 97
Marley, Rita, 7, 8, 12, 17, 19, 24, 26, 30, 31, 32, 33, 81, 87, 94, 96, 102, 104, 105, 109, 110, 111, 115, 117, 118
Marsh, Wellesley, 40
Martinez, Andreas Lopez, 114
Masahiko, Makae, 105
Masouri, John, 29, 39, 151
Maury-Kauffman, Marianne, 73
May, Chris, 9, 10
Mazzoni, Lorenzo, 103
McCann, Ian, 16, 29, 46, 50, 55, 90, 93, 106, 109, 117
McKnight, Cathy, 3
Medina, Tony, 69, 76
Michizou, Miki, 143
Midori, Yamamoto, 106
Miller, Calvin Craig, 40
Miller, Mark, 89
Mitsugu, Shiraki, 106
Monpierre, Roland, 71, 72, 73, 74, 75
Monty, Carlos, 112
Morris, Dennis, 59, 60, 63, 65, 66
Morrow, Chris, 62
Moranetz, Silvia, 94
Moskowitz, David, 37
Moss, Leonard, 122
Moter, Hermann, 118
Motoko, Oshino, 108

N
Nakamura, Naoya, 108
Nappez, Stephane, 76
National Library of Jamaica, 9, 42
Nedland, Sigbjorn, 110
Noa, 105

O
Observer Station, 45
Ojo, Adebayo, 47, 55
Ordova, Jesus, 112
Osei, Gabriel Kingsley, 3

P
Palmer, Byron, 42
Paprocki, Sherri Beck, 36
Paringaux, Philippe, 88
Parkin, Trevor, 9, 10
Payen, Marc, 83
P.C., Marilyn, 111
Pierson, Leroy Jodie, 44, 50
Pines, Jim, 136
Pinn, Anthony, 149
Potash, Chris, 139, 140
Prahlad, Sw Anand, 144

Q
Quilici, Cassiano S., 80

R
Ras Zuke, 145
Reese, Dafydd, 40
Riggiero, L., 99
Riley, Terry, 74, 75, 76
Rooksby, Rikki, 127, 131
Roskind, Julia, 134, 144
Roskind, Robert, 134, 144

S
Salewicz, Chris, 19, 24, 29, 41, 42, 85, 105, 110, 118, 143, 152
Sandman, F.T., 103
Sampaio, Mateus, 80
Sardin, Joan, 115
Schmitz, Werner, 94
Schwaner, Teja, 91, 93, 94
Schwanker, Paul, 94
Selvaggi, Antonio, 81
Sheridan, Maureen, 46, 47, 52
Silveira, Ricardo, 81
Simon, Kate, 64, 65
Simon, Peter, 67, 135
Sloan, Delphine, 89
Sly & Robbie, 149
Smith, Tennyson, 71, 72
Sotheby, Madeline, 9
Steckles, Garry, 39, 40
Steffens, Roger, vii, 28, 30, 44, 50, 58, 60, 61, 64, 54, 67, 120
Stephens, Gregory, 141
St.Pierre, Roger, 8

T
Tafari, Ikael, 144
Taibi, Elisa, 63
Talamon, Brice W., 58, 60, 61, 65
Taubman, Lowell, 41
Taylor, Don, 18, 20, 26, 28, 106
Thompson, Dave, 145
Tiaki, Okamoto, 54, 109
Tobiasova, Sonya, 82

Tosh, P, 29, 62, 82, 97 / Tobler, John, 3
Toynbee, Jason, 36, 37
Truth, Yamakawa, 109
U
Usandizago, Artiz, 79
Uscher, Mitchell, 25
V
Van de Meer, Joost, 110
Vasquez, Montana, 113
W
Wako, Awazi, 108
Walker, Klive, 148
Ward, Margaret E., 15, 84, 118
Waters, Rosa, 38
Watson, Jesse Joshua, 70, 76
Welch, Chris, 18, 21, 46, 118
Wells, Colin, 123
White, Garth, 4
White, Timothy, 5, 6, 7, 10, 11, 13, 14, 18, 22, 24, 25, 26, 33, 60, 61, 65, 81, 82, 91, 93, 101, 107, 111, 115
Whitney, Malika Lee, 7, 8, 12, 17, 24, 26, 104, 118
Williams, Richard, 36, 89, 94, 102
Wilkinson, Juliet delia Ann, 150
Winkler, Anthony, 21, 22, 27, 97
Wint, Eleanor, 29
Wortman, Thorsten, 67
Wynands, Rene, 92
Y
Yamamoto, Yasumi, 104, 106
Yigyeongha, 109
Yoshiko, Gomi, 107
Yoshiko, Oohashi, 105
Z
Zuke, Ras, 145

Publishers Index

A
Acapella, 141
AFA Yavincilik, 117
African Caribbean Institute of JA, 4
African Publication Society, 3
Alamo. 121
Albin Michel, 135
Alternatives, 62
Amistad, 34, 38
Amphora, 111
Anabas, 8
Andrews McMeel, 25
Ankara, 96
Apopira, 95
Arawak, 29
Arcana, 99, 130
Arkiv Forlag, 116
ARS Schibendi, 118
Arthur Baker, 4, 5
Author House, 150
Axis Mundi, 111
B
Back Beat, 145
Balance Arte, 111
Barricade, 20
Beat On Investments, 12
Bilge Kultur Sanat, 117
Bismarocks, 116
Bison Books, 15
Black Rose, 147
Blake, 20
Blandford, 137
Bloomsbury, 19
Blues Brothers, 99
Blues Interaction, 105
Blume, 53
Bobcat, 54
Books Chaka, 104
Book Society of Canada, 42
Bosworth, 49, 151
Buhmann und Haeseler, 94
Burusuintaakushonzu, 108
C
Cambridge Univ., 141
Carib Arawak, 3
Caribeennes, 71, 135
Carlton, 18, 21, 47
Case International, 27
Cassell, 51, 52, 53
Casterman, 85
Catedra, 114
Cauris, 73

Chelsea House, 23, 25, 36
Chicago Review Press, 141, 147
Chinaski, 103
Chronicle, 34, 35, 62
Citelembik Yaylinlari, 117
City Editions, 87, 89
Corgi, 2, 7, 11
Creative Concepts, 122

D

Da Capo Press, 30
Daiei, 104
David Brooks, 66
Distal, 79
D.M.M.P., 60
Double Day Dolphin, 8

E

Edelvives, 113
Ediciones B, 78, 115
Ediciones Sala y Cultura, 82
Editions de Tournon, 51
Editions du Panama, 88
Editions Olms Zurich, 52
Editorial Brasiliense, 80
Editorial Kier, 79
Editori Riuniti, 101
Editor Record, 81
Eel Pie, 59
Eight Companies, 108
Ehapa, 74
Eise Music, 71
Elle U Multimedia, 102
Elm Tree, 5
Encre, 83
E.P.A., 89
E.P. Dutton, 8
Epoch, 59
Excite, 66
Exley, 16

F

Far-Eye, 145
Feltrinelli, 101
Fitzhenry & Whiteside, 11, 14, 18, 22, 24
Flammarion, 90, 148
Florida, Univ. of, 149
Franklin Watts, 75, 76
Fratelli Gallo, 98
Fratelli Spada, 104
Frontline, 144
Fundamentos, 114

G

Gammalibri, 99
Genesis, 64, 65
Giunti, 53, 100, 118, 146
Global Treasures. 64, 120
Greenwood, 37
Grupo editiorial Tomo, 54
Grupo Express, 88
Gower, 42
Grafton, 11
Granada, 6, 11
Gravenhage, 110
Guinness, 138

H

Hal Leonard, 123, 124, 126, 129, 130, 131
Hamish Hamilton, 9, 10
Hamlyn, 17, 21
Hampton Roads, 73
Hannibal, 91, 93, 94
Hansib, 137
Harper Collins, 41
Harry N. Abrams, 143
Henry Holt & Co., 10, 11, 14, 18, 22, 24, 25, 33
Heyne, 91, 118
Holt, Rinehart & Winston, 6
Horizon Illimite, 148
Hors, 52, 84, 87
Hutchinson, 9, 59
Hyperion, 30, 31, 33

I

IMGE, 116
Inconeg, 143
Insight Editions, 67, 68
Insomniac, 148
Interlink, 40
Island, 152

J

J'Ai Lu, 149
Jamaica Media Productions, 13, 14
John Blake, 28
Jucar, 112
Jump at the Sun, 146

K

Kaos, 98
Kawade Shobo Shinsha, 109
Kingston Publishers, 7, 18, 26
Kyle Cathie, 139

L
La Mascara, 112, 113
Lato Side, 97
Lawrence Hill, 152
Lee & Low, 70, 76
Les Arts Avocetta, 80
Les Guides, 86
L'Express, 85
L'Harmattan, 135
Librio Musique, 86, 88
Lieu Commun, 84
Like Kustannus Oy, 83
L'ippocampo, 63
LMH, 26
Longmeadow Press, 15
Lo Vecchio, 100
LuLu, 41, 111

M
Macmillian, 35, 39
Malthouse, 47
Marshall Cavendish, 138
Martin Claret, 81
Marvel, 71, 72
Mason Crest, 38
Menges, 118
Mexicanos Unidos S.A., 110
Minotaurus Projekt, 118,
Mississippi, Univ. of, 144
Modan, 97
Mondadori, 102
Morgan Reynolds, 40
Mosel, 61
M&S, 106
Music & Entertainment, 90
Music Sales, 125, 129

N
National Library of JA, 9, 42
Nuovi Equilibri, 103
Newmat, 10

O
Oceano, 115
Oliver, 61
Omnibus Press, 13, 16, 26, 29, 33, 39, 45, 49, 128, 150
One Love Press, 134, 144
Orion, 36, 42
Owl, 22, 24, 33
Oxford Univ., 137

P
Palmyra, 93
Pan, 32
Panther, 6
Paragon, 20
Parenthesis, 136
Passa Tempo, 96
Peepal Tree, 142
Penguin, 22, 24
Peter Bedrick, 141
Petit a Petit, 76
Pinus, 96
Piper Mainz, 92
Planeta do Brazil, 81
Plexus, 12, 15, 17, 35, 39, 63, 65
Points, 86, 87
Polity, 36, 37
Pomegranate, 17, 24, 62
PPV Medien, 48
Praeger, 37
Press Bureau JICC, 105
Presses de la Cite, 47
Printers Devil Press, 42
Proteus, 136
Pro Verlag, 91
Publication I.D., 122, 125, 126

R
Rasta Cruz, 138
Rastatt Moewig, 118
Raymond Martin, 92
Ricordi Americana, 130
The Rise, 48
Robbin Book, 115
Rock Books, 99
Rockbuch, 94
Rosen Central, 74, 75
Rough Guide, 139, 142, 145
Rounder Books, 44, 50
Route Panos Cigarettes, 95

S
Sanctuary, 48
Savelli, 98
Scali, 55, 89, 150, 151
Schenkman, 12, 13
Schirmer, 61, 139, 140
Schwarzkopf & Schwarzkopf, 67, 94, 146, 147, 151
SeFam, 73
Seuil-Pointe, 84, 85, 86, 87, 118
Seven Oaks, 46
Sha, 107
Shinko Music, 54, 106, 107, 108, 109, 127, 143

Shobunsha, 105
Sidgwick & Jackson, 31, 32
Signal, 39
Sonzogno, 100
Source, 72
Star Book, 3
St. Martin's Press, 23, 59
Strade Blu, 101
Summer Hill, 109

T
Tackey BCI, 4
Tana, 63, 66
Taschen, 40
Taylor Trade, 27
Temple Univ., 140
Three Rivers Press, 34
Thunder Mouth, 46
Tiden Norsk, 110
Todas la Musicas, 113
Tournon, 113
Trinkot, 90
Tuff Gong, 27, 32, 74
Txalaparta Tafalla, 79

U
Universe, 142
Uplink, 106

V
Vent Des Savanes, 75
Ventil, 149
Viking, 19, 21, 24, 56
Virgin, 22
VOSA, 112
Votobia, 82

W
Weidenfeld & Nicholson, 36
W.H. Allen, 3
White Star, 102, 103
Wilhelm Heyne, 136
Wise, 42, 121, 122, 123, 124, 127, 128, 131, 132
World Distributors, 135
W.W. Norton, 28, 58, 60, 65
WOSY, 83

Black and white advert for Bob Marley: Soul Rebel-Natural Mystic, Eel Pie / Hutchinson 1981
From a UK Trade Paper 5.25" x 7.5"

Color advert for Rebel Music: Bob Marley & Roots Reggae, Genesis Publications 2004
From a UK trade magazine 7.75 x 5.25"

Jah Guide

To Be Continued………..